Reminiscing

HYUNA STEWARD

WESTBOW
PRESS®
A DIVISION OF THOMAS NELSON
& ZONDERVAN

WestBow Press books may be ordered through booksellers or by contacting:

WestBow Press
A Division of Thomas Nelson & Zondervan
1663 Liberty Drive
Bloomington, IN 47403
www.westbowpress.com
844-714-3454

ISBN: 978-1-6642-3924-1 (sc)
ISBN: 978-1-6642-3925-8 (hc)
ISBN: 978-1-6642-3923-4 (e)

Library of Congress Control Number: 2021913354

Print information available on the last page.

WestBow Press rev. date: 07/22/2021

Contents

March

April

May

June

July

August

September

October

November

December

2020

January

March

August

September

October

November

2021

January

February

INTRODUCTION

"Hyuna, you told me that you wanted to write a book when we just got married," my husband, Tom, said the other day.

After thirty-five years of marriage, I had forgotten that statement, but I had toyed with the idea of writing since childhood. When I was growing up, my father always said, "Tigers leave their skin when they die, and human beings leave books when they die to leave their legacy."

My mother embraced this motto to her heart, producing eight books after retiring from being an ob-gyn physician. At age eighty-six, she is writing her ninth book. My father, ninety-two, wrote his third book in March 2020. No wonder I am feeling a pinch of pressure to write my book. Notwithstanding, writing has been part of my life ever since I can remember.

I have written my diaries since elementary school. At age twelve, I flew to the United States from South Korea with my two younger brothers, ages six and three, to stay with my parents. They had gone to America one year prior to pursue their medical and political science careers. During that transition I lost my diaries; nevertheless, I still have my journals from my medical school years. When I started my family practice clinic in 1986, I kept diaries of my busy life as a full-time physician, raising four sons with my husband, and taking care of our office staff as well as our babysitters and cooks.

During our children's elementary school years, Tom and I hardly saw each other—let alone had a meaningful conversation. Tom was taking two boys to tennis lessons, and I stayed home with the other two to help them with their homework. Amid this hectic schedule, I wrote small letters and memos to Tom every day, disclosing my thoughts. It was a pragmatic way to communicate my love for Tom, discuss our children's issues, and schedule our social obligations such as going to nephews' birthday parties.

Thirty-five years of medical practice have brought many small appreciative gifts, letters, and cards from my patients. I have written hundreds of letters to these patients to express my gratitude to them. With countless patients, wonderful family, and staff, life has innumerable obstacles. I discovered that I could solve most of these bothersome personal problems through writing: I evaluate an annoying issue, I hash over the controversies, and I make a reasonable resolution. Subsequently, I can move forward to my next conflict.

Through the years, writing became part of my life; the writing was my mental food as well as catharsis. In *On Writing Well,* William Zinsser stated, "Memoir is the art of inventing the truth." The more I wrote, the more I realized the importance of writing to learn and contemplate the evolution of thoughts, manners, and awakening. Stephen Wilbers said, "Writing is a journey, opportunity, for self-exploration, for you, the writer."

As I read different books through my book club, I realized writing does more than tell the history; it also gives inspiration and courage and pictures the most beautiful objects, people, places, and minds. "Writing is one of the highest forms of art," my mother told me; henceforth, she created a two thousand-page novel, *Phantom of Greatness,* a love story set in World War II and the Korean War. However, one big problem that stood in my way of generating these marvelous books: grammar.

This is where my son, Matthew, comes in with his English degree from the University of Toledo. He has been editing all my essays and poems. My mother gave me many books, but the most helpful one was *Keys to Great Writing* by Stephen Wilbers. I have listened to many hours of experts in English on YouTube regarding sentence structure, punctuation, and how to write essays. I received the third-degree black belt in Choi Kwang-Do in July 2018 after eight years of practicing five days a week. I must admit the writing is harder than my karate because the depth of the English vocabulary, creative styles, myriad exceptions to grammar rules, and the coherence and cohesiveness of writing.

I have begun to implement my family tradition of leaving a legacy through my book. I will continue to communicate with my husband, friends, and patients through letters and cards. I will cultivate my life further as I resolve my conflicts through the memoirs by exposing the problems, digesting the issues, and making candid solutions.

E. B. White believed that writing is not just communication. He said, "Communication through revelation—it is the self-escaping into the open."

Stephen Wilbers stated, "Just as writing is self-revelation, developing style is a creative process of self-realization." Through my writing, I wish to convey my values and insights to others as I discover who I am.

I have written my memoir in poems to capture the magical moments, especially when traveling through Canada. I chose poems to grasp the experiences quickly, showcasing their delightful essence. I wrote some stories in poetic form to further expound on relationships and reflect on the beauty of ordinary life.

November 15, 2011

Breaking the Board

I started karate lessons in June of 2010 with my two sons, Matthew and Andrew. I usually work out at the YMCA three or four days a week.

One particular Saturday, the YMCA held an *aerobithon,* inviting all forms of various exercise groups, including tai chi.

I was impressed how tai chi could form the energy from *dantian*, the center of the body. A thought occurred to me: *If tai chi can create that much energy, how much more energy could karate produce?*

Later, I discovered Monroe Martial Arts in Monroe, Michigan, my hometown. I started on June 15, 2010.

In my karate class at Monroe Martial Arts, breaking a board with a front kick was a challenge. For my white and white senior belt classes, I broke boards with front and back punches. During my yellow belt test, I experienced one of the most embarrassing moments of my life.

The karate *do-jang*, the house of discipline, was packed with students
And family members during my yellow belt test.
I passed all my patterns, speed drills, and defense drills.
I just had to break one six-inch wooden board.

As I was getting ready to kick the board,
The head instructor, Mr. Werner,
Told me to use my right back leg
And kick the board as hard as I can.
Using a front kick. This means I was in a left stance with
My left leg in front and right leg in back.

When I kick with my right back leg, the longer distance creates a
Stronger impact, yielding a higher chance of breaking the board.
Letting out a loud *ki-hap*, I kicked the board, but it did not break.
I was embarrassed because the audience's eyes were on me.

The instructor repositioned my right foot and asked me to try it again.
Rivulets of sweat were dripping down on my red uniform, and my heart
was beating a mile a minute. With all my might, I let out a loud *ki-hap*
and kicked the board. I could not believe my eyes. The wooden board was
still in one piece—without even a dent.

My face was red with sweat.
I was mortified and not sure if that sweat was
Mixed with tears. Mr. Werner told me to stop and come back
Next week for one more chance to break the board.
Suddenly, I felt shamefully awkward.

I wanted to try one more time, but my teacher said that he did not
Want me to break my foot with a repetitious kick. At that moment,
I could not have cared if I broke my foot. I wanted to break that
Board more than anything.

However, I had to listen to Mr. Werner; thus, I took the
Whole unbroken board and walked off the stage to the back room
With my head down. I could not sleep that night;
I wanted to break that board in my dreams.

The next day, I asked another black belt instructor what I should
do to break that board. She said I should imagine that I am kicking the
person who is holding the board. This method carries out the continuous

motion of kicking, unleashing the power of that leg instead of stopping at the board.

I couldn't wait another day—and definitely not another week. The next day, I approached Mr. Werner.

He knew what I was going to ask him. He said, "I will show you what you did wrong. Your kicking angle was wrong. You should kick with the ball of your foot in the reverse direction—as if you are pedaling a bicycle backward."

He showed me how to kick on the punching post, and he asked a second-degree black belt instructor to show me the right kicking motion. When that instructor kicked the punching post, he almost knocked down the post. He said, "It is one fluid motion that builds up momentum and power and then unleashes that energy—hence breaking the board."

I tried kicking the punching post as hard as I could thirty to forty times. Finally, both instructors held the board. As I recoiled my leg, I gave off a loud *ki-hap* and kicked the board with all my strength. *Crack.* That was the sweetest sound of the day. The board was physically separated into two pieces. It was a miracle!

I hugged both teachers out of deep gratitude for showing me the right method to kick the board in case I needed to use that kick in defending myself or others. I felt like a ton of indigestion had passed from my chest, giving me a renewed sense of endurance and confidence.

In life, I am faced with challenges every day. It was one simple wooden board, yet it taught me a big lesson to be persistent and not give up.

Finally breaking a board influenced my writing journey. Many obstacles have discouraged me from writing, such as grammar, sentence structure, and unfamiliar vocabulary words. However, as I learned from karate, correcting bad habits and being more disciplined gave me the foundation to create a book. In my book, I have used poems to enhance the meaning of the subject and express the passion and delicacy in a condensed form.

Finally, after four years, I tested for my second-degree black belt.

December 1, 2015

Second-Degree Black Belt

I started karate on June 15, 2010. Three years later,
On June 8, 2013, I received my first-degree black belt.
With intense training, I was going to test for my second-degree
Black belt in June of 2015, but an unfortunate incident happened.

I broke my left pinkie on June 1, 2015. I had never broken
A bone in my life until then. First, it did not seem possible,
But once I could not move my finger freely,
I realized that the damage was done.

The accidental injury occurred when my partner and I practiced
A kicking and punching combat routine. That day, I was wearing
A bigger glove, and the loose fifth finger got caught
By my partner's kicking motion.

"Perseverance and indomitable spirit," our MMA motto, dawned
On me. If I gave up now, I would not be honoring our black belt tenets.
So, here I am, after six months, thank God,
I am testing for my second-degree black belt!

After two months of resting and healing my left fifth finger,
My rigorous black belt test training started by attending the *do-jang*
Five days a week and reviewing patterns, speed drills,
Highest hand and leg techniques, bag fighting, and board breaking.

Although the test took place in December, the studio was warm and
Teeming with students and family members. All the karate tests
Were performed smoothly without major injuries.
Even my left fifth finger stayed intact;
Nonetheless, we needed water breaks.

4

My final test was to break three boards with a
Spinning side kick, using my nondominant left leg.
As I was ready to break the board,
All the instruction ran through my mind:
"Use the spinning speed,
Look and target the center of the board,
Kick it with the heel of the foot."

When I turned and thrust my leg into the board,
"Crack" was one of the most marvelous sounds I've heard.
With my karate journey, I am more confident,
Less fearful of my weaknesses
Of being in the dark, and more respectful and empathetic to others.

I know that I have to learn more martial arts,
But I will always keep our black belt tenets
And ethical codes of MMA in my heart
To make positive changes in my life and the lives of others.

JANUARY 4, 2017

Lost Earring

A couple of years have passed since I received my second-degree black belt.
I have been maintaining my training. Christmas of 2016 has been special
Because my sons and husband gave me a
Beautiful emerald necklace, ring, and earrings.
Those radiant green stones seemed to penetrate my heart with gratitude.

It was an ordinary Friday,
After a half-day at the office,
Generally, Tom and I rendezvous at Red Lobster for lunch.
That day, I decided to wear the emerald earrings, which Tom and
My sons had gifted me as a Christmas present.

These emerald earrings were heavy.
And had a special clasp rather than a tight post on the
Back of my earlobes due to their size.

With a lighter mood, I put the earring on
My right ear and confirmed that the earring was secure.
However, for the left ear, I assumed that I had placed the
Earring on my ear tightly, and I quickly went out the door.

When I arrived at my office, my heart sank when I touched my left ear.
The left emerald earring was missing. I took off my coat carefully to see
If the earring had fallen on my coat, pocket, or sleeve—but nothing!
I could not find that earring anywhere.

My heart was racing at 110 beats a minute,
I took several deep breaths to calm down and go to work.
Since it was almost nine o'clock,
I suppressed my urge to dash out of the office.

My patients' medical visits finished smoothly.
When Tom asked me to go to Red Lobster,
I told him the horrible news about losing my emerald earring.
His face froze for a moment, and he said,
"We'll go home now to look for the earring."
Red Lobster was thrown to the wayside.

We searched everywhere, including the bedroom,
Bathroom, kitchen, garage, and sidewalk.
We went to Matthew's garage, where I usually park my car,
And Matthew's car was still parked as it was that morning.
But nowhere could we find this delicately crafted earring.

Tom suggested going back to the office
To make sure that we didn't overlook
The corners, nooks, and crannies. But all our efforts were in vain.
That night, I dreamed that I was wearing
My emerald and diamond earrings.
I touched the earrings on my earlobes.

The next morning, Saturday, I went to Matthew's garage
To go to my black belt karate class.
In the garage, I noticed that Matthew's car was gone.

I walked around the car to open my red Impala door,
And something caught my eye.
I blinked to make sure that I saw what I was seeing.
It was my missing emerald earring!

I yelled, "Thank God!"
I picked up my lost and found earring, and to my surprise,
It was in the same pristine shape.

It was underneath the center of Matthew's car,
But it was not crushed, stepped on, or damaged.
I picked it up and held it to my heart as if I had found my lost child.

I dashed out of the garage, darted into my house, and hollered,
"Tom, Tom, guess what I found?"
I gently put that treasured earring in Tom's hand.
He was speechless for a moment,
And then he broke out in a huge smile.

Tom and I were in celestial bliss. When we went to St. Mary's Church that afternoon, we were asked to take the gifts up to the altar. We both thanked God deeply in our hearts for this fascinating recovery. "Depend on the Lord. Trust him, and he will take care of you" (Psalm 37:5).

It was a deep faith that kept us going, and the discovery of this
Earring was another of God's deeds.

June 17, 2018

Third-Degree Black Belt

After eight years of karate, since June 2010,
I couldn't believe I was testing for my third-degree black belt.
To obtain a black belt, all students were required to write an essay.
Mr. Werner wanted to see how karate has impacted one's life.

It is ironic that at MMA. where they taught
Powerful and deadly techniques,
I learned the means of self-control. Each karate class started with
A breathing session to clear the mind,
Assess the situation, and focus on tasks.
This mental technique could be used at home,
Work, and in all walks of life.

To obtain a third-degree black belt, I had to break four boards,
Using spinning side kick with my dominant right leg.

I was sweating from performing all the other required tests, and
My heart was pounding in anticipation of the final test.

I stood in a side stance and looked back at the center of four boards.
Suddenly, it became very quiet.
I was drowning out all the peripheral noises.
As I concentrated. I spun and hit the boards with the side kick,
But those boards were still intact.

Instead of feeling shameful,
I took a deep breath to gather my thoughts.
I'd heard a small crack, which meant
One of the boards had partially broken.

I realized that I had kicked too high.
As if I'd fallen off the horse, I quickly remounted it, and
I repositioned in side stance again. I knew what I had to do.
I had to smash the dead center of the board to shatter the wood.

"Look, point, and aim at the center," these instructions
Circled in my head. As I rammed my leg through
The boards, a "crack" sound rang loudly, and
Pieces of wood fell to the floor.

All the tension and suspense were instantly released.
Truthfully, Mr. Werner told us that a person did not
Need to break a board to pass the black belt test.
But everyone felt the triumphant victory
As the board separated into pieces.

Desperation

Desperate wishes are burning inside.
These wishes are all different.
One boy has unrequited love for a girl.
Other person wants to fly a B-2 Stealth Bomber.

We live courageously every day.
We desire earnestly to fulfill our aspirations.
We march forward daily with
Visions tucked deep in our hearts.

A girl is shooting a hundred balls to make the basketball team.
A young man is practicing his guitar for many hours,
Hoping to be a famous musician.
A woman works on a coding project late at night
To climb the ladder in business.
A mother drives her son two hours a day
To his school to give him better education.

We are all desperate people.
We are all backed into a corner, nowhere to turn.
We still move forward, valiantly.
We pray to our heavenly Father for hopeful solutions.

Everyone hears their own beat of the drum.
Everyone perseveres, keeping that flame of inspiration.
Everyone carries that dream and
Steps closer each day.

Toronto, I Feel Like I Belong

When I first came to the United States in 1970,
I felt like I was in a foreign land
With so much blonde hair and so many blue eyes.
I went back to Korea in 1979,
During medical school, for four years.
In Korea, I was one of them, in a throng of
Black-haired people in the downtown of Kwangju, South Korea.

Yet, in my heart, I was not the same person
As I was when I left at age twelve.
I was a twenty-two-year-old immersed in American culture.
For the past ten years, I had felt like an American.
Indeed, I was an American. I just looked Korean.

While I lived in the United States, I just wanted to belong to a group
Or have friends who looked and thought as I did.
However, while I was living in America for ten years,
I did not realize that I was transforming into an American girl.

The Western clothes I bought and wore;
The food I ate, such as hamburgers and fries;
The language of English I spoke;
The American Caucasian friends I played with;
All these daily living, cultural changes gradually seeped into my being,
Helping me feel like a part of this land.

Nonetheless, when I looked in the mirror, I was still not an American.
Whenever I went grocery shopping, to movies, or to college,
I always stood out as being different.
Some days, I wanted to have red hair and green eyes

To be similar to everyone else.
Everyone had big noses and eyes; it was their Caucasian society.

That was America—and most of the immigrants
Were mainly from European countries.
But, I was Asian, and I always stood out
Until I went to Toronto, Canada.
Tom had been taking me to Toronto for vacation
Two or three times a year for five years.
Before that, I traveled infrequently, about once a year.

The changes that took place in Toronto did not register in my head.
I thought Canada was the country where Caucasians were dominant.
When I visited Toronto and Montreal, I recognized that
there were more Asians than Caucasians.
I did not understand how these changes came about.

How were so many Asians living in Canada?
About 60 percent of the people walking around
Downtown Toronto were Asian.
Even more surprising was that Asians were mingling with Caucasians.
People don't even give a second glance when
An Asian girl walks the streets in Toronto,
Holding hands with a handsome Caucasian guy.

I see an Asian man pushing a small baby stroller
With a beautiful blonde wife.
Young Asian girls have transformed into North Americans
With long, beautiful black hair, wearing miniskirts
Or summer shorts with tank tops.
I was walking with my Caucasian husband, Tom,
Holding hands and laughing on Bay or Yonge Street.

As I looked around at my surroundings, I felt like I belonged to this city.
Tom and I are like the majority of people
Who proudly march through this gorgeous city.
These Canadians have accepted the Asian race as their core citizens.

In 1970, I came to the United States.
After forty-eight years of living in North America,
I felt like I finally found the place where I belong:
Toronto, Canada.

August 5, 2018

Meeting an Old Friend, Kay

Walking down the Veteran Park walking path
In Monroe, Michigan, who do I see?
An old friend, Kay. *Has it been five or ten years since I've seen her last?*
She has the same laugh as in our high school years.

She's walking with her sister who's seven years
Her junior, but Kay looks younger.
She still has that happy, vibrant smile.
She welcomes me with warm embrace.
The three of us keep talking, but my husband, Tom, keeps on walking.

Catching up for last ten years, she summed it up in a sentence:
She has her eighth grandchild on the way.
"I am so jealous," I tell her.

She defuses the compliment with her laughter.
I do not sense any remorse about her mother's death.
I have taken care of her mother.

She had carotid vascular disease.
Later, she passed away with atherosclerosis.
I have not seen Kay since her mother's passing.

I wondered if Kay was upset with her mother's death?
I look back to see if I could have done more to save her life.
Her mother was engulfed with an advanced arterial illness.

Even though everything was done properly,
Death is a sore subject
That brings longing for loved ones.

Kay never mentions her mother.
She is immersed in her happy life with her four children and
Seven grandchildren, sweeping off any despondency about her mother.

Now I tell her about my family.
Out of four sons, two sons have gotten married last year.
My oldest son needs a wife.

She tells me that her youngest daughter is not married.
"I'll take any of your children," I tell her.
"You're one of the most respected people in my life."

"You're being a matchmaker,"
She said, laughing.
"I suppose I am," I responded shyly.

We played on a volleyball team at St. Mary's Academy.
I was good enough to make the team,
But I sat on the bench for most of the games.

Kay played as one of the first-string team members
To battle the other schools.
She was one of the nicest players on the team.
Kay laughed away any boast or conceit.

Her humbleness far exceeded her athletic talent.
She gained my respect for her for life.
Short-term kindness goes a long way.

Even a simple gesture of smile, opening a door, or inviting a friend
For an afternoon tea can leave a grateful impression
On another person. Kay is my admirable friend.

Sharapova versus Garcia Tennis Match

Last night, Tom and I watched the Rogers Cup
Tennis Tournament at Windsor on television.
Maria Sharapova played against Caroline Garcia.
Garcia was ranked sixth in the world,
And Sharapova was ranked thirtieth.
Yet all the eyes were on Sharapova.

Sharapova had a more glorious record of five-time
Grand Slam Champion of the world. But she had injuries
And was off fifteen months from the tennis competition.
Now she is back at age thirty.

Garcia was twenty-four years old and from France.
I had never heard of her.
I'd not been keeping track
Of tennis for several years.

First two games, Sharapova from Russia
Came on strong and won.
Then Garcia started to come back with her
Down-the-line shots and consistent deep forehand.

Sharapova's serves were impressive
With 131 miles per hour speed.
She had several ace shots, but they were inconsistent.
She double-faulted just as many times as she aced them.

Garcia's serves were not as pretty as Sharapova,
Because she started her serve from her overhead position.
However, when she slammed that ball, the placement
Of the balls was effective, even at a slower speed.

At least Garcia made more successful first serves.
Sometimes, Sharapova could not return her serves
Due to wide placement. It seemed that Garcia was gaining points
Upon Sharapova's mistakes.

Both players' long, lanky legs showed no cellulite.
Lean, muscular arms and shoulders showed no drapes.
Flat stomachs and smooth firm backs;
They could be models,
Not just the best tennis players in the world.

Sharapova started dragging her serves, and
Her scores were dropping.
Although she still came back
With sharp short-angle shots.

Garcia won the first set, and 2–0 in the second set in her favor.
Her spinning forehand and backhand shots
Were stronger with accuracy.
Confidence was emanating from her face.

Sharapova came back with volleys and overheads.
Not willing to lose without a fight.
Now 4–2, Garcia was ahead.
Sharapova was holding her composure,
Yet her power was slowly draining.

The scoreboard showed 5–3, Garcia's favor.
Numerous deuces with triumphant rallies,
Drop shots, lobbing, overheads, and crushing defeats with balls
Caught in the net or out of line.

Finally, with many second serves of Sharapova,
Garcia took the ball and placed it
Deep in the court, opposite of Sharapova.
She turned her head, but the ball was gone.
The game was over.

AUGUST 27, 2018

EPIC: Getting to Know It More

My staff and I had an EPIC electronic medical record (EMR) for one year.
I am 150 percent better than when I started.
On July 18, 2017, our office launched the EPIC system.
On April 18, 2018, I started to dictate my electronic medical record.

I am much more comfortable using my EPIC.
When three patients show up, I don't panic.
Prepping my chart the day before helps me tremendously.
Mrs. Johnson comes in for her annual physical exam.

She needs twelve medications refilled to three different pharmacies.
My staff fills all her medications at her desired drugstores.
I greet the patient—and I push the button to send her drugs.
Twelve medications are delivered instantly to her pharmacies.

I examine her with an otoscope and stethoscope:
Then, I escort her out to have an ECG and a chest x-ray.
It takes about fifteen minutes to complete her annual exam;
Last August, it took seventy minutes.

I feel like I won a marathon.
I think back to the frustration and agony of
Trying to tackle this colossal electronic monster.
Seeing ten patients a day was a good day.

During the past year, I developed 210 smart phrases for
Diagnosis, symptoms, treatments, and physical examinations.
I put in close to one thousand words in my dictionary,
And I downloaded the EPIC app on my phone to dictate anywhere.

Prepping the charts at home was a huge burden.
Suddenly, my entire weekend was consumed with EPIC.
My eyes were blurry, heavy, and painful.
I purchased new eyeglasses with stronger lenses.

I lost the writers of my charts in the exam rooms with EPIC EMR.
I talk to patients, type, click buttons, and retype.
I peel my face off from the computer, trying to make
Eye contact with patients in between pushing buttons.

Now I am getting comfortable seeing about thirty patients a day.
There were countless times when I could not find
The right medications, labs, and diagnoses.
So many technical malfunctions needed correction.

While talking to patients, the power would go out,
Our staff and I would sit helplessly apologizing to patients.
During the upgrade, EPIC would stop working,
Leaving all of us twiddling our thumbs.

When I started to dictate, I felt like I had wings.
I was barely crawling initially; forthwith, I could fly.
But my EPIC is not familiar with my pronunciation,
So I am constantly going back to correct what I dictated.

Now I am training my EPIC through its electronic dictionary.
I type "constellation," and I say it and save it.
My EPIC is smart—and she remembers my voice and words.
I currently can dictate two or three sentences without correction.

I know that I am still on the tip of an iceberg,
Yet I feel like I climbed the Alps.
EPIC was my worst foe last year,
But she is becoming my friend.

21

Mother

A pioneer and trailblazer
An exemplary woman
Following and accomplishing her dreams

An independent lady
A hard worker, not a complainer
Adapting to her current situation

Direct style
She doesn't beat around the bush
I like that concept

Standing for righteousness and fairness
Compassionate
Empathetic

Believing in God's unconditional
Love and forgiveness
I feel lucky, although, it's tough love at times

Beyond being a doctor
Author of eight books
Leaving her legacy

January 15, 2019

EPIC: Starting to See the Light

After one and a half years, I was beginning to see the light.
Every day and night, sitting in front of my computer,
The drudgery of unending work was lurking everywhere.
I woke up facing EPIC, and I went to sleep with unfinished EPIC.

So many other things I wanted to do, I had to do.
Yet, I was imploding underneath the EPIC chart prepping.
I quit karate in July of 2018 to start writing,
But EPIC thwarted me from writing my memoir.

When we first started EPIC EMR,
We were told that everyone had her work domain
And others could not help one's designated tasks.
Unfairly, the doctor's responsibility increased by 250 percent.

I was swimming underneath the EPIC work pile.
My head was barely out of the water to breathe,
On January 8, 2019, a miracle happened at our office.
My office staff could help me prepping my charts.

My medical assistants could create and open up the charts for me.
God's wonder shined at our office, discovering that
Our staff could create the electronic charts with
Medical histories and chief complaints.

This was another revelation at our office with EPIC.
We could see more patients without much waiting.
I was beginning to see the light;
Maybe I could start writing again.

January 30, 2019

Frigid Weather, Freedom From EPIC

Schools were closed Monday through Thursday this week due to frigid,
Subzero weather in Monroe, Michigan. Even the post office closed for
Two days this week due to Siberian Arctic temperatures. Tom said that
He had never seen the post office closed due to weather in his life.

As with other businesses and schools, our office only opened for half a day
Today, January 30, 2019. Tomorrow, we will close because only
Five to seven people were scheduled. Yet even these people were
Not sure if they would come out to the office due to the chill factor.

Suddenly, we have a four-and-a-half day weekend.
Who would have thought that we would have
This luxurious long weekend?
This extreme bitter climate can bring
Devastation to some, but for others,
It can have the opposite effect of restfulness.

Normally, for the past one and a half years, on weekends, I spent
Twenty to twenty-five hours prepping my EPIC EMR charts.
Since January 8, 2019, my three medical assistants have been helping me
Prep my EMR charts at the office. This is a revolutionary transformation.

I feel as though I broke the chains off my arms
From being enslaved to EPIC EMR.
The past one and half years of bondage to EPIC EMR have been freed.
Invisible steel bars that locked me in the EPIC cage have disappeared.
I feel like an eagle soaring through the boundless sky. Hallelujah!

Heavenly Father has heard my plea and
Unshackled me from this electronic device.
I'm thankful that my three medical assistants can
Help me prep my charts at the office.
They are like my angels providing me rest as if they are giving me
A free ticket to a Hawaiian vacation to swim and walk on the beach.

January 30, 2019 is one of the coldest
Historical days in Monroe County,
But this day has liberated me from the handcuffs of EPIC EMR.
I feel like dancing like Snoopy for snow days, and it would be
For EPIC EMR-free days at home!

February 14, 2019

Valentine's Day Card

Dearest Tom,

Thirty-four years passed since we vowed to each other.
Now, the first few years of our marriage become almost blurry.

I am astounded that you and I sustained our medical practice;
Raised four boys; grew old together.

Perhaps it was your first kiss that infused the flame of love
To kindle our young hearts and feed red ambers to glow.

Your handsome face, I proudly boasted to my friends and the world.
Your blue eyes sparkled and penetrated my yearning heart.

Light sandy brown hair always cut perfect as if you are wearing a wig,
Accentuated clean-cut countenance that resembled Richard Gere.

Your uncalloused hands, which were softer than mine, were perfect
As if they were representing God's admirable artistic creation.

Best of all, I had a sole privilege
To see, examine, and test your pure heart
For the past thirty-four years of our incredible marriage.

Happy Valentine's Day!
My love, my king, my baby.

Your loving wife, Hyuna Steward

Matthew, Our Third Son

Matthew is a vegan. He eats grains and beans,
But he does not eat dairy or honey.
He rarely eats desserts,
Although he indulges in dates and mangos.

Matthew plays tennis.
He coaches and conditions
The St. Mary Catholic Central girls tennis team.
He is a substitute teacher at SMCC High School.

He studies tennis serving techniques on video.
Matthew feeds countless balls to girls.
He shuffles, runs, and jumps on the courts with his students.
His SMCC girls become champions two years in a row.

Matthew plays in the men's tennis league at YMCA.
He teaches tennis to YMCA members as an assistant instructor.
He also takes tennis lessons from Jerry,
The head instructor, one day a week.

Matthew juggles with six to seven balls,
Twirling, circling, and showering them in the air.
He juggles for hours
And people are afraid that his arms might fall off.

There are jugglers at Mackinac Island,
But Matthew can juggle better than them.
With three to seven beanbags,
He throws them high, shoots more, and crisscrosses his arms.

Matthew plays the piano.

When he plays "Clair de Lune,"
The melody melts people's hearts.
His piano music resembles a philharmonic at Carnegie Hall.

Matthew is a writer and reader.
He writes a memoir or journal five hundred words daily.
He edits his grandfather's book
And his mother's short poems.

Matthew has an English degree at the University of Toledo.
He is excellent at writing poems and short essays.
He has received many awards and scholarships for his creative writing.
He is spreading his wings in helping others.

Someday, Matthew may become a famous writer.
He has inherited the writing talent
From his grandparents.
People can't wait to read his published books.

MARCH 9, 2019

Visiting Mom with Diamond Earrings

I appreciate Tom driving us to my mother's house in Toledo, Ohio.
This morning, I called Mom to see how she was doing.
Although her body aches, her muscle spasms are improving.
Now her ankles are swollen from taking Advil four times a day.

I want to make sure that her ankles do not have excessive edema.
The other reason for this visit is that
I want to give her a pair of diamond earrings.
In her poem, "Searching for Light," she lost one diamond
Earring in the sink when she was going
To a formal party thirty years ago.

I want to share a pair of diamond earrings
That Tom gifted me a while back.
My heart is aching for my mother's loss of her diamond earrings.
With Tom's permission, I want to fill that loss with
My beautiful, sparkling, baguette-shaped earrings.

When Tom and I arrive, my ninety-one-year-old father
And eighty-five-year-old mother welcome us.
They are quite concerned about mother's
Recent overwhelming body soreness.

At my mother's house, when I am putting on these diamond earrings,
Her earlobe holes have disappeared from not wearing earrings
For several years. When I gently push the earring post,
Without any bleeding, it finds the previous earring tracks.

Mom seems to be satisfied about wearing those sparkling earrings.
"How do I look?" asks Mom.

"You look like a mother of a queen," answers Tom.
"Your daughter, Hyuna, is my queen, and you are the queen's mother,"

Mom insists on cooking a simple lunch. She has already poured the
Rice in the rice cooker. She wants to make my favorite sautéed squid.
"What can I give Tom?" Mom scratches her grayish-white head
That is formed in a loose bun.

My ninety-one-year-old father's full white hair is
Like a crown, cut and trimmed neatly.
He walks straight, and his lean body appears
Like a sixty-year-old energetic man.
Dad and Tom are conversing about politics,
And with his deep, sharp brown eyes and
Tom's clear blue eyes, they are exchanging topics
Like a ping-pong match.

Mom comes up with the idea of
Making a miso soup mixed with tofu.
Green onions, and garlic for Tom. She also has loose mixed greens
For the salad topped with poppyseed dressing. Mom is happy that
She can spontaneously prepare lunch for all of us within a short period.

Dad and I have a delicious squid dish to our hearts' content as
We wrap it in the roasted seaweed with kimchi on top.
Tofu-contained miso soup washes down our lunch,
Helping all of us with better digestion.

As we are leaving, Mom gives us one package of mochi (rice cake) desserts.
It turns out to be a wonderful unannounced visit to our parents' house.
This surprise visit would not have been possible
Without Tom and his generosity.
I think Mom will cherish those coruscating diamond earrings.

March 15, 2019

Thursday after Work

Driving home, blithe, end of our workweek.
Tom waits for me in our condominium parking lot.
"Kiku sushi restaurant?" Tom asks.
I nod delightfully.

We both ordered Nabe Yaki Udon.
In a soothing clear brown broth,
Seafood, one boiled egg
And scallions are mixed.

Thick white fettuccine-like Udon noodles
Are slurping in our mouths.
Two long shrimp tempura,
Dipped in diluted soy sauce, crunch with each bite.

Tom let me order vegetarian sushi: thirty-six sushi,
Mango, cucumber, and more, are displayed on a square dish.
I drop sushi in my mouth a few times.
The rest of the sushi is packed for our sons, Matthew and Andrew.

Hot steam is misting Tom's face;
His blue eyes have a slightly green hue,
Reflecting from the fine moisture.
Tom and I drink the soup till the last drop.

This is the end of our workweek
And the beginning of the restful weekend.
The topics of our conversation are
Feathery and dreamy like future travels.

Our tacit love flows between us.
Even though silence ensues, there is a deep understanding.
We are creating ostensible sublimity,
Making his love deeper to enlarge my worth.

April 8, 2019

Taking Up the Gifts at St. Mary's Church

Ushers come and ask Mr. and Mrs. Tom Steward
If they would take up the gifts before communion.
"Of course, we would be honored to do so,"
They answer with smile.

In past years, ushers have asked them to take up the gifts,
Many times, if there are not any special events taking place.
It seems as though they are the unspoken designated
Gift carriers during 4:30 p.m. Mass.

This Saturday, the reverend presides 4:30 Mass,
But the deacon gives a sermon.
He emphasizes God being present ubiquitously
At home, at work, in church, and in restaurants.

A mellifluous version of "God's Mercy" is sung and
Permeates to the congregation from the balcony.
The assembly follows and sings, which rises like a
Sweet aroma toward heaven.

Father led, professing that
Jesus Christ died for our sins and rose again in three days.
Through Christ, our sins have been forgiven,
And we have everlasting life.

As people partake in the sacred
Jesus body through Eucharist,
They bow their heads in reverent gratitude
With clasped hands toward their hearts.

Finally, Father makes the
Church announcements,
Father blesses everyone with
"Father, Son, and Holy Spirit, now go in peace!"

March 16, 2019

Movies

Big screen
Resounding sound all around like in IMAX.
Popcorn with pop or juice.
On reclining seats, feet are elevated.

People are ready to enter the magical world!
Lights are dimmed.
People are fastened to the time machine.

June 6, 1944, World War II, in Normandy, D-Day appears with flying bullets as soldiers are wading to the shore of Omaha Beach.

In 1933, four beautiful, talented "little women" are walking in and out of the streets of Massachusetts, written by American novelist, Louisa May Alcott.

In 1939, during the American Civil War, the stunning Scarlett O'Hara taunts Rhett Butler at her Georgia plantation household in *Gone with the Wind*.

Hairdressing

Whiff of perm solution thrusts toward my face
When walking into a salon.
Sitting on a black revolving chair,
The white paste is daubed on the scalp on each row.

After oxidation, the white paste
Converts into an inky black,
Dripping down my forehead.
White square wax papers adhere to it.

While waiting thirty minutes for the color
To absorb to my fading hair,
I turn on the smartphone and go to the Kindle app.
I'm reading a downloaded Tarzan book.

"It's time," she says.
I'm sitting in a chair with my head hanging back into the sink.
A warm shower pours over my head,
And the thick paste is slipping away.

Eyes closed, I'm immersed in the hot spring water.
Time stands still, even better, floating.
She spurts a handful of shampoo on my hair:
Bubbles and foam fill the sink.

A deluge of conditioner spills on my head;
Waterfall floods the hair again.
The heap of hair moisturizer is dousing, and
Finally, she rinses off the velvety solution.

I'm sitting back in the original high black
Revolving chair in front of the mirror:
Different hair moisturizers are sprayed.
The hairdresser is trimming the tips of my hair.

Now the dryer is whirling, blasting, and whipping
With huge square and round hairbrushes.
Hair straightener flattens the fluttering hair.
All the white and gray hair disappears; only shiny, black hair is flowing.

MARCH 21, 2019

Thinking of You

Dearest Tom,

From the first waking moment, who do I think about?
Drinking morning coffee,
Taking daily vitamins,
My thoughts are with thee.

Driving to work,
I pass by you.
Sitting by the exam rooms,
I hear your footsteps.

Walking down the hallway,
I see your smiling face.
My heart brightens,
Generating inner force.

I talk to patients, chat with the staff.
I see you turn the corner;
I feel your presence
Sitting at your office.

When I careen toward my driveway,
I see you waiting for me.
We dine at the same restaurants:
Fish, salad, Reuben sometimes.

"I saw the engine light on in my car," I disclose.
"Let me check that for you right away."
You sense malfunction in my car;
As you feel when things are not right.

In this methodical routine,
We are becoming one.
Your moves, thoughts are embedding my life,
Breath of your love is flooding my quintessence.

MARCH 22, 2019

My Mega Bot

Round automated vacuum cleaner, Mega Bot.
It is the size of my frying pan.
I push the button to turn him on.
He roams around the bedroom, living room,
Family room, kitchen, bathroom, and foyer.

Picking up the dust and hair.
It slides underneath my bed, chairs, and desk.
It stops by the stairs, before falling.
Then it turns to another safer direction.

Hallelujah!
My entire house is freshened up
By simply pushing one button.
Mega Bot is my hero.

March 22, 2019

Windy February

Knocking at the window,
Bending branches.
I-80 is closed.
The Weather Channel is
Advising everyone to stay home.

Whirling wind is braiding the electric lines.
The sky has darkened.
The microwave clock is blinking noon;
The TV screen has blackened temporarily.

A windstorm is fracturing trees.
A gale is lifting papers, even garbage cans
On the streets and main roads.
Many people are fleeing to their basements.

Thank goodness the laundry
And the stove are working.
The shower and vacuum cleaners are functioning.
Despite the howling wind, electricity is operating.

Yet, last weekend, 173,000 people lost power.
The wind is blowing fiercely,
Bringing February cold with it.
Mackinac Bridge is shut down.

In the evening, the wind springs up and
Howls around the houses.
The wind is rushing through the city and farm
Blasting the doors of garages and barns.

One should never underestimate nature.
The raging wind is whisking everywhere:
The wind resembling a tornado is knocking down
The stop signs and billboards.

The shrill whistling wind
Is swaying the traffic lights and
Knocking down the telephone poles.
Darkness emerges into dawn.

Chewing Gum

A cube tropical gum is crunching in my mouth.
Orange juice is oozing out between the molars.
Tentacular sweet buds are vacuuming its flavor.
I'm chomping on its evanescing luscious taste.

Cool sensation, the tropical gum is
Washing away halitosis.
Cakes and doughnuts have been barricaded.
Pounds are dropping.

Multitasking while chewing gum:
Walking, cooking, juggling, and studying.
Blowing huge bubbles that would practically
Cover the face brings back some memories.

Walking home from elementary school,
My friend and I blew bubbles with our bubble gum.
Popping the balloon countless times, yet
We tried to inflate the bigger one each time.

So many flavors: peppermint, pineapple twist, cinnamon,
Spearmint, strawberry, sweet watermelon, and more.
I am trying them after work, on my way
To a grocery store and the movies.
The wintergreen flavor enhances a stroll in a park.

Crushing and grinding gum
Swells my masticating muscles.
Jaws are tightening, biting mucosa at times.
All the flavors vanish; it's time to spit it out.

MARCH 31, 2019

VIA Rail Train, Snow in March

Winter wonderland is dazzling through the window.
The wind is whirling, and clomps of ice are stuck
While they are melting and dripping.
The field is enveloped with a white comforter.
Brown furrowed soil now has countless white lines.

In Harper Woods Junior High School playground,
My brothers, friends, and I created a snowman.
While hurling snowballs, we warmed our hands
With steamy breaths.
But we fought till our gloved hands were soaking wet.

VIA Rail stewardesses are serving fruit trays for breakfast.
Outside, the snow is swirling, clashing, and knocking
On the window to join our breakfast.
Thick brown trees and evergreens transformed
Into pearly silvery landscape.

The train is racing on two steel bars.
In London, Ontario, winter visits them frequently,
As a snowbelt region, even in March and April.
Tom and I are hoping the snow
Has not fully reached Windsor.

March 31, 2019

Riding a Taxi on a Snowy Day in London, Ontario

March 31, looking through the sheer curtain,
White cotton is covering the city.
On all trees, branches, and buds,
The perfect layer of fluffy fleece has perched.

Yesterday, it rained.
Umbrellas were marching through downtown.
These morning cars' windows are
Draped with white blankets.

Icicles on trees create perfect pictures
Like masterpieces in museums.
Pulling out hats, gloves, and scarfs
To combat swirling snow.

A young man is walking on the street
With a T-shirt and an open jacket, shivering.
Knocking on the cab window
Stopped for a red light.

Cab driver is digging into his pocket
To give him some change.
An automated window is opening,
But that young man disappeared.

Delicious Breakfast

Apple and blueberry crepes with whipped cream on top,
And western and Mexican omelets have oozing melted cheese.
Pancakes are stacked as the golden syrup drapes over it.
On the ham skillets, two over-easy eggs are perched on top.

Oh, how I savor these dishes
On Sunday morning at Monroe Grill.
The waitress pours two hot coffees and glasses of water
With a lemon slice floating on top.

Soon the pants are fitting tight;
The belly is pouching;
Thigh cellulite is spreading;
And upper arm drapes are extending.

The menu is taunting me
Like children wanting an ice-cream cone.
Yet are these rich foods friend or foe?
Such a temptation I must face.

Even though the strawberry waffle
With whipped cream is enticing me,
I order oatmeal with raisins sprinkled on top.
Maybe, next time, I will have that delicious breakfast.

April 7, 2019

Hidden Lake Garden

An orchestra of finches and woodpeckers
Are tweeting and rapping on evergreens,
Conifers, and blue spruces,
Welcoming us back this spring.

Tom and I are marching over hills of paved asphalt,
Focused on our strides,
As bushy-tailed squirrels scurry across
The bare limbs of white birch trees.

Brown trunks also stand side by side
Over dry, fallen maple and poplar.
Collapsed logs lay across the beds,
Supporting shades of green moss.

Junipers stretch their arms to shake our hands, those are
Held while shuffling down each steep slope.
We're glad we're not on the bikes
Those often pass, mounting speed down the valley.

The white sun is glowing behind the clouds,
Peeking through dense, overhanging branches.
Packed, naked trees stand tall, but they beckon my coat as
Pachysandras sporadically warm their feet.

Each hilltop reveals the hidden lake
Where our children chased white swans
And fed pinches of bread to fish gathering at the bank.
The fall colors surrounding the water
Are now replaced by packs of coffee-bronze trees.

Toward our homestretch,
Hosta gardens burgeoned baby-green
Stems next to a small pond
Where a duck leaves its rippling wake.

Before Mass

Love your neighbor as much as you love yourself.
—Matthew 22:38–39

A new sturdy brown wooden door opens,
Magnanimous Catholic St. Mary's Church welcomes people.
At the entrance, a circular ceramic tub contains holy water.
People dip their fingers and make the sign of the cross.

High above the altar, Jesus Christ is suspended on a cross.
In the back of the lofty dome, Jesus's ascension among the clouds is
Seen through the huge stained glass.

The light shines through eight long stained glass windows with
Donor's names engraved at the bottom.
Golden chandeliers like upside-down flowerpots,
Bloom light from high up on the ceiling

In the back, several pews are occupied by the same people.
They arrive thirty minutes early to claim their favorite seats.
As soon as they arrive, they catch up on weekly events.
Their faces are beaming as they chatter, turning back and sideways.

Elaine talks to Linda about her recent eye surgery
For a growth, which was benign.
She is recovering but still cannot read books yet.
Bob and Judy are whispering to Ed about their grandchildren.

Carole and her twin sisters turn to the back,
Discussing last week's experience at the casino.
Ushers and other church members greet
People sitting in the last few rows by tapping on shoulders.

April 12, 2019

Purdy's Ice-Cream Bar

Peel the paper off the vanilla ice cream on a stick.
Dip it in the ivory vanilla cream sauce.
When the dripping stops,
It is dipped again in melted chocolate.

After double-dipping in milky chocolate,
It's rolled in the finely chopped almond bed.
Groundnuts are poured over the ice-cream bar.
The cupcake paper is punctured through the stick.

Five dollars has been paid.
Biting into the crunch chocolate ice-cream bar,
Brings back the joy of buying and savoring it
From an ice-cream truck in the hot summer afternoon.

Tom says, "This is the best ice-cream bar I've tasted!"
Sitting by the fountain at the Eaton Center in Toronto.
The vacation is not complete without
Purdy's chocolate ice-cream bar.

Playing Cards with Tom on VIA Rail on Our Way to Toronto

Tom and I are on board VIA Rail toward Toronto.
Sitting back in the reclining chairs,
We look at each other holding our smiles.
Is that a hint for the gin card game?

Tom is shuffling and distributing cards.
"I am going out with five."
"Are you kidding me, you got me with thirty-five points!"
Tom exclaims.

"Gin!"
"What! You caught me with a handful of cards."
"Fifty-four points? Wow! Might as well give up now,"
I despair.

Shuffling cards in silence,
Trying to focus on our next move.
Flipping the cards from the main deck and
Exchanging them for favorable cards in our hands.

"Who's winning?" the stewardess asks,
Breaking our concentration.
"Oh, my husband is winning,"
I answer, startled.

Soon, we see the skyscrapers of Toronto.
All of our competition is dispersing,
Erasing our sore losing and winning streaks.
Thrilling Toronto is waiting for us.

VIA Rail Train Ride from Toronto to Windsor in April

Passing by the bare trees and boughs
Like a fast-forward cinema.
Raindrops inching on the VIA Rail windows.
Sparse houses and vast meadows emerge.

Whistle blowing, the train is slowing down
To stop at the Woodstock train station.
Expecting hippie crowds wearing
Beads and headbands as in the sixties,
But only an handful of ordinary people get off and on.

On yellow pasture, several geese are feasting on the leftover grain.
The soil has been tilled to sow soybeans and corn.
On the murky sky, dreary clouds are floating.
Dense trees are connecting earth and sky down the horizon.

Lonely telephone poles are linking
Thin electric wires, keeping the
Communication and power intact.
The red blinking gate is coming down.

VIA Rail is running through the brown steel.
This is a different view than two weeks ago,
When the earth was covered with snow
Coming home from London, Ontario.

Coco

Coco likes tuna.
Coco is shy and hides when people come.
But he likes to play
With a bell tied to a string.

Black mixed with white fur
Runs swiftly up and down the stairs.
Padded paws are silent,
Moving quickly like a shadow.

Bright green eyes
Are talking to me.
"I know who you are,
But I haven't seen you in a while."

Coco runs and lays next to Ashley, my daughter-in-law.
Sometimes he perches on the top
Of a couch, and licks, combs
Andrew's, my son, hair.

When Coco was just a baby,
I used to give him an airplane ride
In a box walking all over the house.
Now he treats me like a stranger.
Many months have gone by since I last saw him.

In the morning, Coco is a second alarm clock.
When Andrew's alarm goes off,
Coco is scratching the door to make sure he is up.
But when Andrew goes to the bathroom,
Coco jumps in bed next to Ashley.
Coco is like a little child wanting attention.

When Andrew or Ashley come home,
Coco is by the door. "Meow, Meow,"
Welcoming and telling them
How much he missed them.

He longs for their petting and cuddling,
But he enjoys eating more.
He wants to get down to the serious
Business of a wet meal of beef or chicken.

Tom and I dine at Kiku, a sushi restaurant in town once a week.
We are thinking of our grand-cat, Coco.
Now we buy two rolls of tuna-avocado sushi.
Thinking of Coco indulging in tuna brings a smile.

Today, Matthew, my other son,
And I brought tuna sushi to Coco.
When Andrew, Ashley, Matthew,
And I ate on the dining room table,
Coco hopped on the chair and craned his head.

"I want to eat my favorite tuna."
Coco gestured, looking at the rows of sushi.
Andrew pulls out the raw tuna from the sushi,
And he gives it to me to feed Coco.

"Give me five, Coco," I say holding
Tuna in the other hand.
Hesitantly, but eventually
He gives me his paw,
Tuna is given for his reward.

Food is an excellent way to teach cats.
Five of us all dined together for the first time.
Coco is our first grand-cat and grandchild.
Laughter, teaching Coco to high-five,
I can see that we'll have many more
Tuna-avocado sushi suppers.

April 19, 2019

Orange Jam Sandwich

Each half-pear wedge of avocado
Is sequenced side by side
Over a slice of a multigrain,
The surface spread even to its
Edges with creamy peanut butter.
Both halves are kissed tight
With orange jam.
Its gloss, my firstborn,
Its shade, a warm twin of
Half-moon tangerines
Plucked from their globe.
Arranged alongside my twice-bitten lunch.

Carole King in Toronto

Cool, lively on King Street, ambulance siren is blaring.
Tom and I are walking hand in hand
Tracing our way through black coats
And the occasional red scarf.

Old and young with fashionable attire,
Hundreds are flocking to Princess of Wales Theatre
To kindle the passion for Carole King's
Songs from the 1960s and 1970s.

Carole King's play of her life and music
Was inspiring and transforming.
Her lyrics and songs touched millions of hearts
Making many number one songs in the USA.

After she was married at age sixteen, she and her husband
Only wrote songs for other singers and music bands.
They had two daughters, but eventually
The marriage ended up in a divorce.

Carole King needed money to support herself.
With the lyrics that she has written,
She began to sing.
To her surprise,
Her songs were an instant hit.

Her beautiful voice, appearance,
Contemporary theme,
And a genuine message to youths and adults
Caught on like wildfire.

Laundry

Separating dark and light, warm water is pouring out.
The green liquid is swirling. A washing machine is twisting,
Swooshing, spinning, and completing the rinsing cycle.
Wet, damp garments are dumped into the dryer.

Whirling, cycling heat, and clicking zippers and buttons
Are rattling against the metal wall.
One hour of incessant tumbling and flapping,
Warm, fluffy vestments are pulled out of the dryer.

Piled robes, uniforms, and dresses,
How tedious and boring is the folding task.
One can easily give up and run out to the tennis court,
But start stacking and placing them in drawers.

Depression can be overwhelming:
Lying around, lacking motivation, and accumulating chores.
Like folding laundry, start with one task at a time.
Picking up the crumpled shirts, the pile is diminishing.

Go take a walk, call a friend, and clean the room.
The day seems to be brighter, and the mental fog is lifting.
Look at the shrinking heap of garments,
Thoughts are clearing with less cluttering contemplations.

By solving a small problem at a time,
No longer is melancholy, anger present.
Soon, all the jumbled clothes disappear;
The linens and pants are neatly gathered.

April 27, 2019

Eggplant with Bean Curd Dish at Windsor

The gourmet dish was brought out at Rose Garden, Windsor.
It appeared like a feast fit for a king.
Large chunks of eggplant and triangular tofu
Mixed with dark brown sauce, it was a picture-perfect dinner.

Purple luscious piece melted in my mouth.
Hot fried bean curd tasted
Better than P. F. Chang's.
I savored every bite with white rice.

It is the same dish that I order at
Chinese Sizzling in Dundee, Michigan.
But they have a different sauce, ginger-garlic.
To me, they both taste superb!

I wished that I could take the rest to Matthew.
It's his favorite dish; unfortunately, we are in Windsor.
As we stroll back to our TownePlace, Marriott Hotel,
We wonder what we will try next time.

APRIL 27, 2019

Raining in London Ontario, Canada

Raining, pouring down to earth,
Over buildings, trees, and roads.
People walk with umbrellas or hoods on their jackets and coats.

Dundas Street is under renovation.
The whole street is torn up,
Mounds of dirt and pebbles
Strewn along with old broken black pipes.

New brighter orange pipes are lying around
To be used underneath the ground.
A torrent is drenching all the backhoes
And caterpillars, halting their refurbishing project.

On King and Richmond Street, gusts are wicked,
Almost blowing people's umbrellas inside out.
But these umbrellas can be used
As shields from the tempestuous wind.

A continuous stream is flowing relentlessly.
Tim Hortons and Starbucks are packed,
Waiting for the gushing to stop and the
Rainbow to emerge.

Coffee

Coffee is a universal language.
Distinctive aroma awakens everyone.
In the US, Canada, Korea, Germany, France, Italy,
Eyes open as the brewing coffee
Wafts through the atmosphere.

In restaurants and trains,
"Qu'est-ce que voudrais café?"
"Oui, merci."
Hot steamy coffee brings out smiles.

Coffee is the best friend in the morning
Like sunny-side-up eggs for breakfast.
Coffee catapults the day with vigor.

MAY 2, 2019

On Our Way to See Our First Grandchild

What does it mean to be a grandmother?
I am thrilled.
I am lucky.
I am old—more responsibilities.

Is this child a girl or a boy?
Am I spoiling this child
With dolls, toy cars, or an iPad?
There goes my bank account.

It's a surprise.
It's a blessing.
How will I feel when I hold this baby?
Will it bring back memories of my four sons?

I wonder if I have to retrain myself
To hold the baby.
Am I going to pinch myself,
For it not to be a dream?

Am I going to smile, cry, or laugh?
My heart will bloom at this precious.
I will say to her or him,
"My joy, my sweetheart."

Trucks

Large rectangular vehicles with
Lights in the front and back such as
Single or double FedEx trucks are
Running on the highway.

Countless trucks are delivering
Food, mail, Amazon goods,
And so much more
From the east to west coast.

Some are hauling stacked new cars.
Others carry used trucks on their backs.
Trucks can also block the view for a little Fiat or Malibu.
But at times, trucks can pave the way for them.

Passing trucks brings shaking and whizzing
As if dwarfs are running next to giants.
Sedans can weave through traffic
Better than enormous trucks.

Yet respecting each other's
Strength and weaknesses,
Sharing freeways in harmony
Brings everyone home at night.

MAY 12, 2019

Misty Mountain Hills

Cats' eyes flow through tortuous roads.
Each peak triumphs the thick curtain.
Distant cars emerge like ribbons
Of ants heading home.
Sparrows evanesce evergreen
As we plunge into the vapor.

Highway

Charging on I-75, heavy traffic runs on six lanes:
Three lanes moving forward,
Three opposite.

Highway is like our fast-paced lives;
Once the trajectory is chosen,
One cannot turn around.

Driving with the flow,
Cars are whizzing by right and left,
Propelling to the next destination.

A wrong turn, one can astray for many miles.
In life, the wrong decision can cost
Relationships, fortunes, and health.

Running on I-75, the driver's eyes are
Converging on the road.
One slip, and the damage is too massive to recover.

Living the Dream with Tom in Montreal

The Notre Dame Basilica gathers a crowd.
A musician is singing;
The guitar case opened to throw in coins.

Tom and I are walking on St. Xavier Street.
Instead of asphalt, blocks of
Cobblestones are for walking only.

Horse carriages are roaming
Old Montreal as its history
Unfolds through the driver.

Montreal, mini Paris, is so far away from home,
Yet, so near to our hearts;
Our second home, we yearn to visit each year.

We see restaurants on every corner.
Tom buys me a mint chocolate chip ice-cream cone.
Fifty degrees, nonetheless, Montreal ice cream is tasty.

Tom and I dance away Friday night at Le Balcon to sixties music.
We twist our hips, stomp our feet, and clap our hands.
We relived our thirties with "The Heads" musicians.

We enjoy a spaghetti lunch at Rosie's, although it was
Not as good as Mrs. Pezzino's homemade pasta dish.
We watch *John Wick, Aladdin,* and *Hustler* movies.

Walking down St. Catherine Street
With multicultural citizens:
I feel like I belong to this group.

March 6, 2020 (June 2019)

VIA Rail Train 5:50 a.m.
toward London, Ontario

Door opens at 4:45 a.m. at the VIA Rail Station in Windsor.
Tom obtains parking tickets from the inside kiosk.
The outside kiosk is disconnected.
Amid dark, chilly air, dragging our luggage
Through the parking lot, silent parked cars greet us.

Bright lights awaken us inside the VIA Rail Station.
Tom purchases two tickets to London, Ontario.
Two familiar staff, Marc and John, welcome us with bright smiles.
The empty train station is quickly filled with
Crowds of multiple ethnicities,
Yet the courtesy and politeness are admirable.

At 5:30 a.m., Tom is looking at his watch
The VIA Rail train is taking off on time like
Big Ben in London, England.
Now coffee is poured.
"Bonjour, Bievenue!"

Dusk is gradually lifting against azure sky.
Feathery coral clouds are reflecting from dawn.
Half a fireball is emerging from the eastern horizon
Painting the sky crimson and orange.
The train is running toward London,
Chasing the rising sun.

June 1, 2019

Thunder

A loud clash resonates by my window.
Did a heap of trucks collide?
There seems to be a heavenly war
Blasting cannons at their opponents.

Is the earth quaking?
Flashes of lightning brighten the inky night.
Should we run down to the basement
Or curl up under the blanket?

Thunder is nearly shattering my windows.
Is God mad at us?
Warriors may be riding chariots of clouds.
They are crashing into each other, creating
A "ba-boom" calamity in the sky.

It is best to go to bed,
Hoping in the morning
The thunderbolts will disappear,
And the golden sun may smile at us.

Toronto Layover

Coming from Montreal
In the business lounge,
Overwhelming fatigue shrouds me,
I can hardly open my eyes.

Drinking a latte and a Canada Dry
For an energy boost.
Tom is charging his iPhone, 73 percent charged.
In thirty minutes, hoping to be over 90 percent.

On this trip, Tom forgot to bring his
iPhone charger, a rare phenomenon.
Usually, I am the one who forgets
The iPad, a dress, lotion, etc.

Tom is filling his cup of coffee.
So many choices: latte, cappuccino, cafe mocha.
Tea: green, Earl Grey,
English breakfast, and much more.

Many men and women in business suits
Are patiently waiting on leather couches or
Black swivel chairs, talking on their phones,
And working on their computers on marble tables.

Granny Smith apples piled to the brim
In a basket for passengers.
A huge round clock with a gold rim
On the south wall is ticking away.

Soon, an announcement is heard through the speaker.
"Train 71 to Windsor is now boarding at gate 17."
Briskly we're rolling our bags toward the boarding gate,
Dreaming of a hot pasta lunch in the spacious VIA Rail seats.

Almost There

White and yellow lines marking the
The surface of gray roads.
Parted trees are welcoming
Streaming cars and trucks with their green arms.

Traffic is picking up as we approach Philadelphia.
Cars are cruising around 76 miles per hour.
Tall mountains are barricading the highway.
A Penske truck is coming from the opposite side.

A flock of eagles is circling over the highway,
Looking for scraps of food to break their fast.
Overcast clouds are floating in the eastern sky
Threatening with rain or storm on this beautiful sunny day.

Our GPS is fastened to our front window's inner corner.
It says that we'll arrive at our destination in forty-five minutes.
Tom is humming a song as he keeps an eye on the road.
One long channel of cars is running on this asphalt.

The speed limit is 70 MPH,
People are driving from 62 to 74 MPH,
Keeping steady flow, trying to make
It to work on time.

Tall, ancient trees are boasting their natural green cloaks
To people who work in the skyscrapers.
Tom says, "We have thirty-five minutes till we reach the Marriott."
It's not so bad for having driven nine hours.

June 16, 2019

Dinner at Kiku

Goldfish are swimming in a large tank,
Disappearing behind Matthew's ears as he scans the menu.
Seaweed is hula dancing in the water
Welcoming people to the restaurant.

Six of us are sitting around the table.
Andrew is discussing his plans
For relocating for his job in six months.
Matthew will be
Teaching tennis during the summer,
After finishing coaching tennis for
SMCC high school students in the spring.

Thomas is smiling with the recent sale
Of his apartment last month.
Tom talks about politics
And the upcoming election.

Thomas orders three tuna avocado rolls,
Between illegal immigration and foreign trade.
Matthew is having mango and
Cucumber rolls for his vegan diet.

Andrew orders three cucumber avocado rolls
Without sesame seeds due to his allergy.
Tom always orders his favorite
Seafood Nabe Yaki Udon Soup.

Tom loves this dish; not only is it delicious
But also healthy, and it is not fried.
Tom tells his sons that he stopped watching
Evening news out of frustration.

I order the jumbo shrimp hibachi dinner.
The fried rice accentuates sautéed vegetables.
Ashley Marie will be celebrating
Father's Day this evening at Cracker Barrel.

One hour evaporates quickly as our
Tummies are full from nonstop conversations.
Many birthdays and special occasions, such as Father's Day, were
Enlivened at Kiku with cheers and camaraderie.

First Day of Summer in London, Ontario

Clear sky, only a few clumps of clouds are floating.
Seventy degrees, the sun is radiant in London, Ontario.
Shorts, sandals, and tank tops are emerging everywhere.
Convertibles are cruising; people are sitting on patios of restaurants.

Tom and I are walking on King Street, hand in hand,
Shades are on like *Men in Black*.
The sun is beating down on our faces and arms.
The soothing warmth is penetrating our souls.

We walk to Victoria Park for the food festival.
Multicultural cuisine of European chicken,
Barbecued ribs, Indian samosa, and
Korean beef, Bulgogi, are displayed.

This event reminds us of our Monroe County Fair
In August of each year.
That is when we eat elephant ears and funnel cakes
With cinnamon buns and chewy taffy.

I indulge in mango bubble tea, and
Tom savors the chocolate-caramel ice cream.
In the afternoon, we watch
Men in Black at the Imagine Theatre.

Fighting with aliens, using
Powerful nuclear weapons.
This time, woman in black
Are introduced.

Thank goodness, these men and women are
Good officers of the galaxy, promoting peace and harmony.
Into the light, we plunge again. Walking more than twelve miles a day.
Soaking the sun, warm breeze tickling our faces.

Tom and I in London, Ontario

Ambling through the streets of London, Ontario,
Wearing sandals and short-sleeved shirts.
Perfect warmth entertains us in the sun,
In the shade, a cool, light cardigan breeze.

Walking on Dundas Street,
Museum of London, Ontario arises,
Bringing memories of several years back
As we look through giant windows
At countless trees and a brook.

Stopping at Covent Market Place,
Suddenly bustling with people
Selling and buying muffins, soups,
Sandwiches, coffee, and tea.

Outside, local farmers are proudly
Displaying their strawberries, cucumbers,
And homemade loaves of bread.
Barbecued marinated chicken and
Burgers are wafting in the air.

June 27, 2019

Father

You sacrificed your bright future
For your children's fruition.
You gave us fishing nets for life
Through education.

Preparation was the key to success.
Repetition was instrumental in achieving a goal.
You valued the physical activities as much as studying.
You watched us like a hawk.

You inspired me to write my book.
You have not denied me any of my necessities.
I still remember your resounding voice like Tarzan,
Echoing on top of the hills after hiking with you in Korea.

Your muscular strength was wonderment through a child's eyes.
You taught brilliant theses as a physics professor.
University students surrounded you with admiration.
Your unwavering love will never be forgotten.

Bob Evans Before Going to the Hidden Lake Garden

Driving a Rolls-Royce on M-50,
Canadian radio station CBC is on
With Angeline Tetteh-Wayoe,
Playing the latest popular music.

Tom parks in his favorite parking spot,
At Bob Evans in Dundee, Michigan.
Tom and I walk in; the waitress, Terri,
With auburn hair, says, "Welcome back."
She sits us in the middle plush booth.

Another waitress, Becca, smiles at us and
Brings out two cups of coffee with extra creamer.
Tom orders his usual: "Rise and Shine."
I order two strawberry crepes.

Tom says, "We've come a long way,
But I am happy way we are."
"I would not want any other way,"
I chime in our conversation.

"Our four boys seem to have found their niche,"
Tom places his soft basted egg over the grits.
"We should continue to guide them to right direction
As our parents did for us."
I bite into my strawberry crepe
With sips of hot coffee.

Before the burning sun beats down
On the last day of June,
Tom is cruising toward Tecumseh
To hike through the forest of Hidden Lake Garden.

July 1, 2019

Tunnel to Canada

It's hard to imagine we're underwater.
The radio took its last breath
Before falling silent.

White-tiled walls reflect even
Strobes of spellbound light.
Two flags emerge side by side.

My eyes narrowing in wait for
Faint whispers of anthems among
Echoed engines wheeling single file
Toward the surface.

July 4, 2019

VIA Rail to Toronto

In July, plants are burgeoning.
Flourishing trees are welcoming us to summer in Canada.
Verdant grass, soybeans, and corn are sprouting.
A church steeple is standing tall in London, Ontario.

A lonely caboose decorates Glencoe Station.
Dilapidated car parts fill the Chatham junkyard.
A sunny sky is covered with lambswool,
Underneath, the river is flowing over a small dam.

Silo standing in the meadow of wheat,
Where horses are grazing.
Sporadic castle houses are peeking
Behind crowded tree branches.

Crossing the bridge with tall, V-shaped metallic rails
The train is running underneath,
Graffiti expressing their thoughts,
Woodstock, a train station, but no one boards our car.

Stacks of woods and cement are
Anxiously waiting to be used
In scattered capacious factories.

The children's playground is decorated with swings and slides.
This brings flashbacks of our children
Playing at the Kiddie Korner Preschool in Monroe, Michigan,
Wanting to be pushed on their swings and
Catch them when they slide down the silver slide.

At 8:16 a.m., the breakfast has begun on the VIA Rail.
The tray cart is rolling down the aisle.
The train speed is picking up to 60 or 70 MPH.
Coffee is shaking; Toronto is waiting for us.

July 5, 2019

Tom and Me, Canada Vacation

Thirty-five years ago, on August 11,
We were wedded.
My parents and Tom's brother-in-law
Introduced us through the grapevine.

Tom and I worked hard,
And bought a house.
We filled it with four sons who ran around
The house and clambered the trees in the yard.

We leased a GMC Suburban and packed our children;
We drove to parks, orchards, museums on weekends.
Twice a year, Tom drove to Canada
Niagara Falls and Sea World in Ohio.

We climbed the Clifton Hills of Niagara Falls.
Ripley's Believe It or Not Museum dropped our jaws each time.
The children played Skee-Ball to amass a bagful of tickets
To exchange for plastic keychains.

After graduating from colleges, our sons
Moved out to apartments and
Managed their financial affairs.
They have introduced their girlfriends to us.

Two enraptured weddings brought families
And friends together for a celebration.
Oh my! Tom and I are grandparents this year.
Our beautiful grandson brings unfathomable joy!

Our chicks found their nests.
We have seen *Come from Away* and *Mary Poppins*.
The VIA Rail Train is whisking us to
Montreal, Toronto, and London.

Our Favorite City: Toronto

Walking on Bay Street, 77 degrees,
We're basking under the sun.
Wearing our black shades,
My black hair is flowing in the wind.

Passing through city hall and
Nathan Phillips Square, ten-feet-tall TORONTO
Letters constructed with cement are standing
For children to crawl, sit, or stand on.

Following the throng of people,
We turn right on Queen Street.
Tank tops over mini shorts
Shout out summer.

In our sixties, are we dreaming?
Toronto in July is bewitching us as in our thirties.
We chatter our children's affairs with laughter.
Our favorite restaurants are tossed in the air.

Two hours evaporate
As we are immersed in the story
At the Cineplex Theater
On Yonge and Dundas Streets.

Containing 235 stores, Eaton Center shopping mall
Completes our more than ten thousand steps a day goal.
Sale signs are everywhere; young ladies and men
Wearing trendy outfits weave in and out of stores.

The last day, we stroll through Queen Street;
The sunset etching this magical moment in our hearts.
Sadly yet longingly leaving Toronto,
Only to come again soon.

Tom

You have lifted me from the dungeon:
You threw a lifesaving rope.
Tightly, I wrapped myself around it.
Gingerly, you pulled me up.

The light of hope shined to my forehead.
I was buried under the books,
But you enchanted me to other parts
Of the world via rails and freeways.

In searching, groping in the dark,
"Where are you?" I shouted to
Gleaming stars and a moon
In the vast dark galaxy.

Angels heard my cry and
Brought you to my doorstep.
Timid, naive we were;
Trusting God, you held my hand.

Thousands of letters written
To win your heart.
"I love you," you whispered into my soul.
Your breath enlarged me as a universe.

My loneliness has faded away.
Dreams were transformed into reality.
The love as strong as life is being
Ingrained into our hearts and spirits.

July 26, 2019

Tom in Toronto

The sun shone through the eastern sky.
On your pledge to love me, I looked forward
To the moon to strengthen all those bonds,
Which seemed to make a lasting marriage

You entered my life without a word.
I sit beneath your glance, as children do,
With souls that tremble, from an unwavering
Yet extravagant inward happiness.

Ah, keep near and close, your dovelike soul!
And when my fears rise,
With your broad heart, surely
Encircle my inadequacy.

I hear your voice and vow,
Perplexed, uncertain.
Beloved, is that you?
Or did I see all the glory as a dream?

I think of you! My thoughts do intertwine.
Each day seeing and speaking to you is like
Flower blooming through the morning dew.
I am the vine concealing your trunk.

Morning Aerobics

Ann, Betty, and Tom
Lay their steps
Like people claiming pews
At church.

Yawns and waking nods
Paint the front
And back mirrors,
Fading to Cathy's music.

Feet shuffle to the
The rhythm of ponytails.
Knees and legs soar
Like Broadway chorus girls.

Two lofted ceiling fans
Breathe relief into
Gentle stretches,
Ending in prayer pose.

AUGUST 8, 2019

Fog on I-80 in Pennsylvania

Hazy fog mirage
Appears like a lacy curtain.
I am curious:
What's on the other side?

Cars are cruising
Upon the hills.
Bosky thick forest
Fencing the I-80 highway.

A distant gray mountain emerges
On the murky horizon,
Infusing its peak and the sky.
Driving for copious hours.

Layers of ridge are
Hidden behind the mist.
Clouds are intercepting the sun—
Yet, lucky that it is not raining.

August 20, 2019

Swimming on Saturdays

A man with black trunks
Drowns me in a
Wake of thrashing feet.
Blue and red circles
Strung like candy necklaces
Keep my backstroke
Straight enough.
Through goggles,
A haze of colored flags
Float overhead.
It's enough to pretend
Like I'm ascending the Millennium Force
As my lungs tighten.
Anything to shrink the
Clock and my cellulite,
Finishing with ten more laps
Of breaststroke before a
Long, hot shower.

Colorful Hidden Lake Garden, May 2019

Green leaves cloak
Countless trees.
White Petals of crab apple blossom
Flutter along the path
As scattered yellow
Daffodils smile at us.

Tall trees arching high
Above interlock their arms.
Violet flowers line the asphalt's
Edge, batting their petals.

Down the hill, pink tiger lilies
Crane their stems toward
Footprints and cattail bulbs
Strut from the ditch in the soft wind.

Painting the Sky

Two cyclists are spinning wheels by the highway.
Tall, cross-shaped wooden telephone poles are
Standing by M-50, connecting electric lines.

On a huge powder blue canvas
White and gray clouds are
Hurled and jettisoned.

Floating cotton candy
Beckons me to grab them and taste.
Flying dogs are appearing.

Rabbits are running on a blue tarp.
A dragon is spewing fire out of its mouth.
A striped fish is swimming.

A turtle is inching on the azure vault.
A poodle is chasing a cat.
The strolling elephant magically appears.

As Tom's Rolls-Royce runs on the highway,
Dynamic views of different pictures
Are changing on the gigantic cerulean sky.

August 29, 2019

VIA Rail Sunrise

A crescent orange ball is rising,
Permeating its coral light.
Darkness is transforming into
A bright morning.

A colorful fireball is emitting
Blinding light to the earth
From the galaxy as it
Rotates our solar system.

Circular tangerine light is migrating
Slowly toward the midpoint of the sky,
Transmitting its warmth to plants,
Animals, and human beings.

The VIA Rail Train is running,
Chasing the sun like an
Olympic champion climbing the hill to
Light the torch.

Montreal on Labor Day Weekend

Montreal on our tenth year,
Cotton wool clouds are floating on a vast canvas.
We walk through Old Montreal on cobblestone streets
With feathery spirits, glancing at familiar restaurants.

Suzette's Boutique catches our eyes—
Warm pleasant memories are flooding.
Oh, how beautiful was that orange matching outfit!
We hike on the downtown square.

Cartoonists and venders are selling cards and bracelets.
Ice cream, gelato, and smoothies are enticing the crowd.
An Italian opera singer's melody permeates the park;
She wears a long black dress with spaghetti straps on the back.

Every day, a different singer occupies that spot,
Entertaining a throng of people.
In turn, the audience throws coins
On their open guitar case for appreciation.

A new dainty restaurant by Notre Dame Basilica
Nourishes us with a pizza piled with mozzarella.
The spinach-walnut salads are tossed down
With an old-fashioned bottle of root beer.

Horse carriages are parading through the town;
Guests are listening to the history of Old Montreal with awe.
The Science Center and IMAX Theater are beckoning
Us to visit by the St. Lawrence River.

Tom in Montreal

On our twenty-second Montreal trip,
How do I express my love?
I love you as an ordinary girl
Who loves hiking Montreal Park with you.

I love you when we walk down the
St. Catherine Streets.
Hand in hand, confessing
Our love for each other.

I love you like a queen of the world
As you make me be.
As we ascend the escalators,
I gaze into your clear blue eyes.

I love you from my soul
When we watch the US Open
During the quiet night. Our love flows
Through these captivating moments.

I love you as we stroll down the
Cobblestone Streets of Old Montreal,
Dining at Rosie's Italian Restaurant
And sharing flatbread pizza.

I love you while we share
The Dairy Queen Dilly Bar and
Blizzard Ice Cream by the
Contemporary Museum Park.

I love you as we watch
The chess players
On the street using
The life-sized chess pieces.

I love you every day
And on special vacations,
For we are young at heart,
And love is timeless.

September 2, 2019

VIA Rail: Changing Trains in Toronto from Montreal

Cloudy, gray sky,
It's raining and nippy outside.
Soybeans and corn are soaking up the moisture.
Trees are dancing while hydrating their bodies.

Lonely brown telephone poles are
Bridging electric lines,
Running next to a train
As a marathon running mate.

Sheep are grazing in the green meadow.
White-spotted cows are meandering in the field.
Cylindrical hay bales appear picturesque.
The Ontario River is scintillating next to parallel iron rails.

We must make a connection in Toronto—
Seven minutes are allowed to make a switch.
Wearing a backpack, holding my purse,
And digging for my luggage under the piled bags.

The PA announcement is made.
A stewardess is turning the key to open the train door.
Tom and I are dashing out the steps to the next train on the left.
Within five minutes, we are on board a train to Windsor.

"Hew, that was stressful to make a connection within seven minutes,"
Says a lady passenger who sat behind us.
"I know. That was a close call," I tell her, letting out a sigh.
"Now we can resume our card game," Tom says, laughing.

September 7, 2019

Topspin

At least a hundred balls blanket the
Soldier and Sailor Park tennis courts in Monroe, Michigan,
Surrounded by yellow evergreen needles
From the trees that line the fence.

An older couple is playing tennis on the third court.
We choose the first of the
Four courts with tree shade.
Matthew is feeding me forehands to perfect my topspin.

Wearing a US Open cap and sunglasses,
My fingertips are going numb.
Matthew has been teaching tennis this summer.
He is adding topspin to my forehand.

When hitting a steady feed,
The ball spirals to the other court.
But when we rally fast, I push
The racket, creating flat balls.

Now we are back to square one,
Hitting one ball at a time,
Focusing on brushing up and over.
Only a thousand more balls
To commit this to muscle memory.

Bianca Andreescu versus Elise Mertens

The small ponytail of brunette hair
With pin clips, the black sun visor is shading her brown eyes.
She is wearing a purple and black
Sleeveless shirt with a matching tennis skirt.

Nineteen-year-old Bianca Andreescu,
From Canada, is playing
A semifinal match for the
First time at the US Open.

Elise Mertens, a twenty-three-year-old
From Belgium, has played
In several major worldwide
Tennis tournaments.

Elise has a colorful, flowery
Matching outfit.
Her braided blonde hair is tied
On top of her head with light pin clips.

Topspin forehands are hitting short sharp angles.
At 100 miles per hour, Elise serves to place the ball
Deep by the service line.

Elise won the first set, 6–4.
Bianca coming on strong,
Winning the first game of the second set.
Now she volleys short, impossible to reach for Elsie.

At 3–3 in the second set,
Elise shoots the down the line with her backhand.
Bianca turns her head,
And the ball whizzes by.

Bianca drops the ball over the net,
And Elise luckily picks it up high.
Bianca finishes the game
With a powerful overhead.

They both win a set.
On the third set,
The pressure is so intense
One could cut it with a knife.

Elise serves with a wide-angle ace.
Long deep rallies entertain audience.
Bianca hits the cross angle, and
Elise hits the ball into the net.

On their faces and necks,
Sweat is rolling down due to
Physical and mental stress.
But their eyes are sparkling
To win the next point.

Arthur Ashe Stadium in New York
Is hot and humid.
After each game,
A fresh towel and new balls are
Fetched by young boys and girls.

Bianca is requesting water as her
Energy levels seem to slowly drain.
Elise is maintaining her composure,
Thinking of her next move.

The audience is biting their nails,
At 4–5 in the third set.
The players' forehands and backhands are flawless.
Their hearts are pounding.

Both girls are bouncing before receiving serves.
Bianca throws the killer shot, hitting the white line.
The audience cheers wildly for
Her triumphant victory.

SEPTEMBER 18, 2019

Kavi Humbad, Our Grandniece

Happy Birthday, Kavi.
One year flew by like a whirlwind.
But ask your dad and mom;
They will tell you every milestone.

You are walking.
What an enthrallment.
Last time at Grandpa Shah's,
You were crawling across the floor.

Each time you cried, Mom fed you her milk.
Jar food introduced new flavors.
Now sitting at the table with family,
Sharing solid food, wonderment.

Your beauty is emerging everyday.
Sparkling brown eyes,
Sculpted perfect nose,
Rose petal lips—God's amazing gift.

Happy Birthday, Kavi.
May you continue to blossom
As a healthy, exquisite, charming girl
Who brings endless laughter and joy to your household!

Love,
Great Uncle Tom, Aunt Hyuna, and all the family

Fly in St. Mary's Church

Tom is shooing the fly off his face.
Bob is sweeping his hand in front.
Matthew, a young man, is swatting his shoulder
To scatter the fly that's buzzing in his ear.

Fly is now encircling my nose.
I tried to catch it with my right hand.
It flew off again.
Father is speaking at the podium.

His accent is strong.
Are people distracted, struggling to understand Father?
Perhaps, this fly is bothersome, and
It is hard to focus on the reverend's homily.

Hands are flinging up at the front pew,
And to the side and back of us,
Trying to divert the fly.
No one dares to kill a fly in church.

The sermon is reverberating,
People are smacking the fly in the air.
Father is raising his hands toward heaven.
Is anyone listening to Father's homily?

October 3, 2019

Rain at Windsor

Rain is stomping on the roof of the VIA Rail Train Station.
Pouring October rain is unusual,
Yet cars and people are drenched.
The parking lot is becoming a small river.

Tom is glad that he does not have to drive
Four hours to Toronto in this wet environment.
Raindrops are hitting against the window,
As if they want to come inside the building
To wipe themselves dry and catch warmth.

Perhaps the sky is shedding its tears
For people's transgressions.
Farmers and trees need rain.
People prefer not to have soggy rooms.
"It messes up my hair," ladies would say.

OCTOBER 6, 2019

Departure Morning from Toronto

"We gotta go, so we can come back,"
Sad, but delightful words Tom throws out.
Cramming sandals, makeup bag, and jeans,
Into my black luggage, struggling to zip.

A taxi drops us off to Tim Hortons near the train station.
An eye-opening scene is viewed as we walk in at 5:30 a.m.
With a long line by the counter. Fresh doughnuts are
Not yet made; cinnamon rolls and hot coffee will do.

October Festival in Toronto gathers a young crowd
As well as some rough fans yelling
Rude language. Mostly yawning faces are
Leaning on the table over their backpacks.
Rolling our luggage in the dark, misty morning,
I feel a light shower on my face, yet not enough to drench my hair.

The huge VIA Rail building is empty except for
Security guards patrolling the beige square-tiled floor.
A stark contrast to Friday 6:00 p.m.
Where countless people are hustling everywhere.

At gate 21, a middle-aged bearded man with a paunch,
Wearing a VIA Rail badge attached to strap around his neck,
Is pulling the metal stand to make a temporary
Corridor for economy passengers.
His face mundane, another Sunday-morning job
Perhaps he needs a hot, steamy coffee.

In twenty minutes, a mile-long line is formed.
We've been there, economy section, for the past ten years.
We traveled with our four sons, standing first in line,
For two hours early in the morning.

Now people stare at us as we sit in the business-class section.
Little do they know our history.
An announcement is made for the train
Departure to our destination: Windsor.

We are climbing up the escalator first.
A deluge of house tasks is looming in our heads.
Unforgettable plays and movies,
Scrumptious Korean and Italian dishes, and walking in the sunny streets
In Toronto are quickly fading in our memory.

OCTOBER 24, 2019

Visiting Egg Smart

Early Saturday-morning dusk is lifting,
Yet the sun is still hiding.
Street-dusting car with twin brushes
Sweeping mud off the sidewalks,
Like a shaving brush at the barbershop.

It picks up McDonald's brown bags
With half-eaten french fries.
Tom and I are strolling toward
Our favorite breakfast diner.

Familiar Greek middle-aged waiter,
Short black haircut, beard shaved clean,
Greets us, "Welcome back,
You can sit wherever you want."

This is the deli where we discuss our oldest son's
Nuptial suitors and youngest son's food and
Tree allergies while dining on sunny-side eggs,
Curry sprinkled potato squares, and rye toast.

Each time we're in Toronto, we visited
The Egg Smart, for five years, keeping the tradition.
Simple happiness is shared, and the wrinkles on our faces
Deepened from laughing in this restaurant.

OCTOBER 24, 2019

Koreatown in Toronto

Strolling through Koreatown in Toronto,
Beauty shops and Korean restaurants filled the streets.
Grocery stores and markets exhibit sundry frozen fish,
Fresh fruits, and gold fish-shaped cakes filled with
Sweet bean paste baked at the store in a gridiron.

For a moment, it seemed as if I was walking through
My hometown, Kwangju, Chonnam State, in South Korea.
A grandmother in a bun is roaming in the market with a grocery bag;
A middle-aged Asian man is displaying
Scrumptious strawberries in front of his store.

A young girl with long, black hair,
Wearing tight leggings, is talking on her
Cell phone as she marches through the
Construction zone lined with orange cones.

Tom and I are checking out the best authentic restaurants.
Pictures of Korean dishes are displayed on their
Windows, yet the places do not appear the cleanest.
Tom finally picks one restaurant with
Vines covering the window panes:
Their spotless tables meet with Tom's satisfaction.

Tang Su Yook, fried beef with sweet and sour sauce, and
Chajang Meon noodle dish with black bean paste are
Out of this world. Next time, we'll order lunch-sized meals.
On our way out, Tom notices a picture of Kimchi—the
Kim's Convenience TV series actor—our favorite show.

The owner tells us that the *Kim's Convenience* cast dined
At their restaurant regularly before they became famous.
Our hearts are swollen to have eaten lunch
Serendipitously where our admired
TV show thespians enjoyed Korean ambrosia.

Tarzan

Powerful
Chivalrous
Handsome
Superb physique
Chief of a gorilla tribe
Speed
Swinging on the trees
Raised by ape mother, Kala
King of the jungle
Protecting Kala with his life
Fighting with truculent gorillas
Hunting fierce lions and cheetahs
Keen eyes tracking spoor
Extraordinary hearing of lions' footsteps
Perceptive olfactory nerves detecting species
Seeking justice in the human and animal world
Warm heart
Discovered treasures
Carrying on heredity, Greystoke in England
Loves Jane Porter

NOVEMBER 2, 2019

Detroit River

A natural river between two countries: USA and Canada.
From Windsor, majestic high-rises,
Including the Renaissance Center and
GM Headquarters, are standing tall in Detroit, Michigan.

From Detroit's side, Caesar's white dome
With green windowsills and turrets along the Ford offices,
The TownePlace Marriott building where Tom and I stay
After crossing the tunnel occupies Canadian soil.

The flow of the river provides water
Resources for both countries.
Two countries are connected by
A two-mile-long bridge above and a tunnel below.

They are sister countries,
Sharing a similar culture, food, and wardrobe.
Tom and I cross over the Detroit River
More than sixty times a year to visit our sister country, Canada.

Hidden Lake Garden in November

The dense forest has remodeled to
Orange, brown, and yellow,
Covering its floor with a
Warm bed of titian.

Birch trees are standing naked
With bare branches. Clumps of
Tangerine-colored leaves are clinging to boughs,
Hoping for no rain or gusts.

On oak tree barks, beige mushrooms are sprouting.
The bed of sparse pachysandra is
Vining its tendrils around the tree trunks,
As it does in my father's backyard.

Mystic dark timberland is now
Transparent only with lanky wildwood.
Standing tall, spreading its cantaloupe-
Colored cloaks on the ground.

Hidden Lake is oscillating by
A gentle breeze gleaming with
Sunrays blinding birds
Flying over the lake.

Coffee ground-colored trees
Surround the lake,
Telling the hikers
Another season has passed.

Tom's Coat

Dark brown coat,
He wore it for three years.
In Eaton Center, Toronto,
Browsing through Hudson Bay.

New designer coats are displayed
A mile long, twitching Tom's eyes.
Tom is trying a black double-layered
Winter coat.

A salesman comes
And zips his coat
With a smile.
Tom peeks at the price: $875.

Tom gently takes off the coat and
Politely moseys over to the next aisle.
His arms ache from peeling
Off countless coats.

He goes back to the
One he enveloped himself in the first time,
Eyes catching the price: $112
Beige with thin, black-checkered lines.

Deep pockets with tight snaps,
Now his keys and visa
Won't fall out of the pocket.
Puffy down collar hugs his neck and body.

He walks out of Hudson Bay
With a satisfactory grin.
He drops off his old warm coat
At the side door of Trinity Church.

The next day, a homeless man is
Dancing in Tom's winter coat.
Tom's heart feels warm and cozy,
Seeing this vagabond's surprise bliss.

Black Sunglasses

Where did my sunglasses go?
I had them yesterday, I am sure,
And two days ago, at the Rose Garden restaurant in Windsor.
Accidentally, I pulled out my black sunglasses instead of my
Reading glasses to read the menu.

On Friday at VIA Rail, Tom thought he saw my sunglasses,
But I only used my reading glasses to read my books.
On Saturday morning, as we walked the London, Ontario, streets,
I did not wear my sunglasses because of the somber, gloomy morning.

We saw a movie, *Ford v. Ferrari* at the Imagine Theater.
Of course, I did not use my sunglasses.
I searched my luggage and my purse, unzipping every pocket.
As if a ghost thief had grabbed them from my blue purse,
My sunglasses were nowhere to be found.

Tom called the TownePlace Marriott in Windsor,
And I called the Rose Garden, but the results were in vain.
We enjoyed another movie, *Midway*, about Pearl Harbor.
To leave no stone unturned, after the movie, in the busy lobby,

I talked to one of the staff who received tickets for incoming customers.
"Excuse me, do you have a lost and found?"
"Yes, we do." He turned around after he directed the
Last person to the right movie theater.

"What do you need?"
"Did you see any sunglasses?" I asked as my heart was thumping.
"What color?" he answered nonchalantly.
"Black."

"Yes, I have them right here. We found them yesterday.
Were you here yesterday?"
"Yes, we were here. We saw *Ford v. Ferrari*."
He opened the drawer in front of him.

He pulled out my black sunglasses.
I saw stars. I was flabbergasted.
I wanted to give him a huge hug and even a kiss.
Then he turned around and grabbed the next person's movie ticket.

Tom looked at my black sunglasses like a precious gift from the angels.
Yesterday, when we were watching *Ford v. Ferrari*,
I must have dropped my sunglasses from my small blue purse.
That blue purse was soon replaced by a deeper-pocketed black purse.

Caramel Apple

The basement of the Eaton Center is occupied by a food court.
The chocolate factory offers Granny Smith caramel apples.
We are mesmerized by the flowing chocolate fountain.

For years, Purdey's double chocolate-dipped
Ice-cream bar was our dessert at Eaton Center.
Tom lost twenty pounds by shaving calories and ambulating.

This year, a Granny Smith apple
Covered with chocolate,
Replaced Purdey's ice-cream bar.

Tom gave up the best ice-cream bar.
Would a caramel apple satisfy his sweet tooth?
Tom and I took a chance and bought it
Paying $11.30—and they even sliced it.

Each bite broke through the walnuts, caramel, and
Milk chocolate. At last, the sour Granny Smith is mixed
With deluxe sweet creamy texture.
Tom will never go back to the Purdey's ice-cream bar again.

December 1, 2019

Train from Toronto to Windsor

Massive steel is moving on time.
Wheels rumble in the inky morning,
Double windows are rattling,
The wind is whistling.
Swishing windows when
Passing by another train.
Stopping at the Oakville;
A grandma gets on board
With roll-on luggage.
The train trundles as it starts
Toward its next destination.
Cimmerian sky transforms
Into grayish-blue, gazing through
The tangled tree limbs.
Hot coffee aroma
Opens passengers' eyes.
Beyond the steel tracks,
Someone waits for them.

December 1, 2019

Jump Rope

In the high-intensity interval training class in Monroe,
The instructor, Michelle, is hopping with a jump rope.
"One minute, go for it,"
She shouts as she twirls the rope.

My two feet are in the air
Up and down like pistons.
I see the narrow alleys in Korea.
On the small cemented ground,
Two small feet pounded the earth
With a long rope and two handles.

"Round two, one minute
For the cardio workout,"
As the instructor's words ring in the air,
My two feet are alternating
One foot after the other.

There are many small hills in Korea,
But there are not enough paved roads for marathon running.
We used jump ropes in school and the neighborhood
To accommodate the limited space in South Korea.

"Third round, everyone, be a superstar!"
Michelle encourages while she encircles her black rope.
My feet are leaping as I did with my cousin
In my youth, turning in circles within the jump rope.
Two friends are whirling the rope at each end.

Playing with jump ropes was the main
Fun game after we decided who was
Going to spin the ropes using
Rock paper scissors.

"Fourth and the final round, give your best,"
As Michelle's command hits the air, the YMCA HIIT class
Members carry on their final jump roping.
My feet hop, skip, and dance with
The thick plastic rope, finishing with a double jump.

Shower

Streams of warm water are deluging down my face and body.
After sweaty aerobics class,
A hot shower is heaven-sent.
I close my eyes—I am floating in the warm Pacific Ocean.

White foamy lather crowns my head and mixes with my black hair.
Balmy water washes down all the grease and dust.
It feels as if I am being baptized in holy water,
Leaving me feeling clean and renewed.

The pleasant shower envelops my skin and soul,
Quickly purging all the external dust and dirt.
Yet, it feels as though my spirit is being purified.
I have not taken a bath in a whole year.

The lonely bathtub lures me to jump in
With the Jacuzzi, water massage, attached to it.
But a fast, silky downpour blessing
From above is hard to resist.

January 19, 2020

Snow in Toronto

Saturday morning, the weatherman has been
Announcing a forecast for snow.
Tom and I take a taxi to the Distillery District in the morning.
Light flurries softly touch the ground,
Yet some melt away, leaving bare streets.

As we entered the Soulpepper Theatre,
A snowstorm ensues.
We wait out the storm for five hours,
And then we open the main door to exit.

Wow, ten inches of snow blanket the village.
It feels like *The Lion, the Witch, and the Wardrobe*,
Changing from autumn to winter,
As one opens the magical door.

Now people bundle themselves with hats,
Scarves, and boots.
We are trudging through thick piles of snow,
Holding on to each other to avoid slipping.

Toronto has been camouflaged as a fleece-white city.
The cars are careening and sliding;
The snowplow and salt trucks are
Emerging everywhere—but not fast enough.

People say the north has a lot of snow,
But I would not have believed it if I had not seen it
With my own eyes. What a difference five hours has made,
Transforming cosmopolitan Toronto into a snowy Siberia.

Our Marriage

He said, "I will marry her," to his cousin, yet he has not seen me.
We are from different continents: Asia and North America
He may like blondes or brunettes, but I have black hair.
Tom has blue eyes and sandy light brown hair.

My eyes are dark brown.
I grew up with Korean tradition.
He is used to American culture.
Tom attended Catholic Central High School.

I attended St. Mary's for the last two years of high school.
Yet I was still embedded in Korean customs.
I did not go to prom, but it did not bother me.
There is no prom in Korea.

The first time, we met at my parents' dining room.
After our second meeting, my parents asked Tom
If he wanted to marry me. He imagined the cartoon with
Wheels in his feet dashing out the door.

Yet, he stayed calm and said, "Yes, I will marry her."
He drove me to the airport to fly to my
North Dakota family practice residency.
He proposed to me on the phone in two weeks.
I said, "Yes, I will marry you."

In five months, we were married at St. Mary's Church.
We honeymooned in Minnesota, so we could make it to my
North Dakota family practice retreat the following week.
We had four sons.

After thirty-five years, we celebrated Tom's sixty-fourth birthday
With children and one grandson.
Love grew minute by minute, day by day, and year by year.
We are bound by the inseparable ties with a vow that rings till eternity.

MARCH 12, 2020

Spinach

Bundles of fresh spinach
Thrown in a boiling pot.
Limp spinach leaves are rolled in balls
Squeezing out all the water.

Sprinkles of salt, soy sauce,
Roasted sesame seeds, and
Chopped scallions are mixed.
Sesame seed oil is glazed.

In my mother's warm kitchen,
Heaping the green spinach dish
Has accompanied white rice
For the many decades since my childhood.

Indulging the savory spinach,
Brings out Mother's mystical,
Enchanting taste in our
Mouths and hearts.

August 21, 2020

Jet Express

The speedboat to Put-In-Bay,
Half an hour of thrills on Lake Erie.
Cool waves gently move,
I want to reach out and dip my hand.

A green line of islands flanks the lake.
Speedboats are skimming,
Trailing whitecaps and foam
Like in a car wash.

The Davis-Besse Nuclear Power Station stack
Is pluming out incessant smoke in Port Clinton, Ohio,
Burning and creating energy.
It reminds me of the twin Edison stacks in Monroe.

Three layers of the deck: first floor with a ceiling,
Second floor is a half ceiling that is halfway open,
And the third floor opens to the sky.
Everyone is wearing a mask, but they don't stop talking.

In the distance, boats are engaged in
Fishing, cruising, and parasailing.
Calm Lake Erie stretches out to the horizon,
Till it touches the sky, which blows feathery clouds.

Put-In-Bay is approaching,
And some of the past presidents have visited.
Rattlesnake Island and Bass Island are appearing.
Perry's Monument—at 352 feet—is observed as a lighthouse.

I can picture Commodore Perry
Sailing toward the British ships with his
"Don't Give Up the Ship" flag soaring
During the War of 1812.

The staff is opening the front-side door to get out to the deck
And fasten the boat on the cemented anchor.
Alighted, Tom and I are rolling our rented orange bikes
On Delaware and Catawba Streets in Put-In-Bay.

August 22, 2020

Dawn

The breakfast room lobby looks out
To Lake Erie through
Huge glass windows and doors.

An early-morning continental breakfast is ready.
As I was pouring the plum tea, mauve-gray dawn is rising
From the eastern sky through the dusky morning.

The calm lake stretches out till it meets the sky.
Pale pink lights with two seagulls
Gliding against the horizon.

An elderly man wearing a cap is watching
The dawn with his coffee cup by his side.
Gentle waves are creating a musical melody.

Another middle-aged man sits on the wide
Cement border of the hotel and eats an orange,
Viewing the panoramic lake as the sun rises.

I am floating,
Watching the violaceous dawn
That matches my raspberry yogurt.

A Placard for Dad

The phone rings.
Dad hit a parked car.
He wants the placard to park his car in the
Handicapped zone.

He asks his ophthalmologist,
But his eyesight is too good.
Dad asks me to sign the License Bureau paper
To allow him to obtain the placards.

Tom and I drive to my father's house the next day.
I call the Ohio License Bureau
For the placard requirements
"He will need doctor's prescription for it," the staff says.

Unfortunately, I did not bring my prescription pad.
Without any grumbling, Tom drives me to my office in Monroe.
On our way back, torrential rain is pelting our windows.
The highest-speed windshield wiper is not fast enough.

In half an hour, we are picking up my father
And speeding toward the Ohio License Bureau.
Tom decides to wait in the car.
My dad and I walk up to the office.
It is an eye-opening sight.

In the office, all six feet of distanced chairs are occupied.
And there is a long line outside.
A pleasant lady is directing everyone.
She gives us a D-626 ticket for our turn.

Another customer asks, "How long is the wait?"
"Over one hour."

"I am ninety-three years old; can I have a chair to sit down?" Dad asks.
"Of course, sit down here please."
A chair is provided immediately.
Within five minutes, the lady leads
My father into the air-conditioned office.

"He'll be all right; you must stay outside until the next chair is available,"
She explains apologetically.
After fifteen minutes, she leads me to a chair,
Six feet away from my dad.

A middle-aged man in a uniform,
About a fifty-year-old brunette lady with a walker,
A teenager, long brown hair, tapping her toe,
And mid-thirties-young man are all wearing masks and waiting.

My dad joins the crowd and patiently waits.
Two weeks ago, he and my mother waited four hours to renew his license.
I read the Ohio placard license form again. It requires the duration.
I add August 28, 2025, five years, to my prescription.

I recall dad pulling me out of a religious group,
"Word of God," at the University of Michigan.
My strong father has always protected me and guided me to the right path.
I trusted him to steer me to become a family practice physician.

My father has been the beacon and fortitude of my life.
Sitting and waiting with him is my pleasure and privilege.
Reminiscing about my father's countless helping hands,
The one and a half hours evaporate like seconds.

Italian Entrée

Mrs. Pezzino calls my office in the morning.
"Could you have Dr. Steward stop at my house after work?"
I ring her doorbell,
Mrs. Pezzino greets me in her summer dress.

She is cutting the Italian zucchini that she picked from her garden.
I roll up my sleeves and help her dice peeled potatoes and zucchini.
In the boiling pot, with olive oil, tomatoes, onions, and basil leaves,
She adds cubed potatoes and zucchini from a container.

While waiting, she slices the eggplant and scatters salt over it.
In a huge wok of heated vegetable oil,
She fries the eggplant until it's brown and crispy.
"Hyuna, take out the large pan and boil water to cook our pasta."
She boils the pasta perfectly—not too crunchy and not too doughy.

"Many years ago, your mother and I made tomato sauce
After we picked tomatoes from my garden.
This is why I called you."
She had a close friendship with my mother.
They were neighbors and best friends who shared weekly events.

Mrs. Pezzino and my mother arranged my wedding
While I was away in North Dakota for my family practice residency.
They booked the church, reception, sent invitations,
Chose flowers and a photographer.
Tom and I showed up for our wedding with three hundred guests.

"I wanted to make you and your son, Matthew, an Italian dinner.
Mr. Pezzino loved this soup and pasta;

He wasn't much of meat eater," she said fondly.
Her husband passed away five years ago.
They were married for fifty-four years.
Tom is jealous of Mr. Pezzino:
"He lived like a king with the best Italian entrees."

On my pasta, she even sprinkles the mozzarella enhancing the taste,
Like a five-star Italian restaurant in Toronto.
Finally, the steamy soup is ready. The potatoes and zucchini
With thick, pink creamy soup's rapturous taste sends me to the moon.

Her long-term friendship with my mother extends to me,
Making her the godmother of my son, James, and my "second mother."
Her devoted Christian faith shines on her face
With daily reverent prayers.
She is a dear friend and a spiritual adviser.

Pecan Pie

A doorbell rang.
When I opened the door,
A pie container was sitting on my doorstep.
In the driveway, inside the van, Alan and Vonnie waved at me.

During COVID-19, we could not get together
Once a week at a restaurant
As we had done past several years.
Vonnie surprised Tom and me and baked a pecan pie.

It was warm; it had just come out of the oven.
We sliced a large portion for each of us.
The chunky, crunchy pecans mixed with caramel
Wrapped in flaky pie crust were magnificent.

Alan was the best man at our wedding.
He and Tom, my husband, attended the same high school.
When we dined once a week, all those memorable stories
Spilled out, making everyone laugh till tears rolled down our cheeks.

When the coronavirus hit the US and the world,
Our get-togethers stopped—just as with all families.
Vonnie and Alan have been getting takeout meals,
As we have, for the past six months due to COVID-19.

Vonnie surprised us with two pecan pies.
The heavy ceramic containers were almost as beautiful as her pecan pies.
Upon returning her pie containers with watermelon and honeydew melon,
She gifted us with homemade face masks for coronavirus prevention.

We can't wait for our weekly dinner get-togethers
When the COVID-19 vaccine becomes available.
We long to share our family events, hilarious anecdotes,
And laughter, maintaining our perpetual priceless friendship.

Golden Hill

As we climb the Hidden Lake Garden,
Golden leaves decorate the hill.
Once-verdant shades are now brilliant yellow,
Reflecting the radiance of the sun.

The garden is cloaked with
Saffron curtains that brighten the forest.
Poplars and ferns have transformed from
Green and orange to gilded wardrobes.

The beauty of nature
Reminds us of the circle of life;
Fading ivory hosta leaves
Are wilting and withering.

When we hike through the woodland,
The floor has metamorphosed to a titian bed.
Four deer galloping down the ravine,
Bewildered seeing strollers on a footpath.

Leaves are fluttering like Montgomery butterflies
As the breeze tickles the autumn foliage.
The Hidden Lake reflects the picturesque
Background of fall timberland.

NOVEMBER 27, 2020

Pneumonia

The day before his birthday, October 28, 2020,
Thomas told me that he had a
Low-grade fever and slight sinus congestion.
With COVID-19 lurking around us,
We decided not to have a family get-together
For Thomas birthday celebration.
Basically, he quarantined himself for the next ten days.

We communicated through phone calls, but his fever did not subside.
In fact, his fever reached 101 degrees.
I told him that I would prescribe him
Zithromax, antibiotics. He still was not coughing, but when the fever rose,
He was having cardiac palpitations, headaches, and copious sweating.

In spite of antibiotics, his fever was climbing
To 102 and 103. Tom, my husband, and
I suspected that he may have COVID-19,
And we dropped his food by his door.
On November 5, I left his favorite pepperoni pizza
By the door. He appeared
To have glassy eyes, a pale face, and a frail body
That seemed ready to collapse.

The fever had been like a roller coaster,
Making him feel like he'd been hit by a truck.
His brother, Matthew, said, "You can't let a fever fry his brain like that!"
Finally, after ten days of battling with a fluctuating fever of 99 to 103,
I suggested to Thomas that he go to the ER.
Thomas did not argue with me.

I called the ER doctor to let him know that
Thomas was coming to evaluate his fever.
At the ER, his fever was 103, his heart rate was 119,
And his blood pressure was elevated to 150/95.
But his blood test showed normal WBC, and
His chest was clear with an oxygen level of 97 percent
However, the chest x-ray showed bilateral pneumonia.
The COVID-19 test was negative.

The viral infection panel showed *rhinovirus,*
Which is usually responsible for simple *cold.*
Even though Thomas had a normal white count
And an oxygen saturation
Of 97-99 percent,
With an unrelenting fever and bilateral pneumonia on chest x-ray,
He was admitted to the hospital.

When the infection specialist was consulted,
She still suspected COVID-19.
She kept Thomas in isolation and started him
On an IV of Levaquin to cover possible atypical
Pneumonia of mycoplasma or pseudomonas.
Thomas' fever would go down in the afternoon,
But it would spike during the night and the morning.

Doctors even added an IV of Cefepime and
Vancomycin to broaden his infection coverage,
But his fever did not capitulate.
By that time, he had taken his fourth COVID-19 test.
All the results were negative, leaving the
Doctors in a dilemma about the causes of fever.

The nurses and kitchen staff were wonderful.
They gave him his oral and IV medications on time
And provided 7-Up and sandwiches for his nausea.
The doctors' communication was excellent

Through phone—even during a Saturday night.
Despite all their efforts, Thomas fever
Continued to rise to 102.8 degrees.

Now doctors were looking into fungal, atypical viral,
TB, or even far-fetched tumors.
Four days into his hospital stay, a CT scan of chest,
Abdomen, and pelvis was ordered at 6:00 p.m.
Since he was in isolation, I could not visit him.
He was staying on the third floor with other
Isolated COVID-19 patients.

I texted him around 5:30 p.m., and he had not
Had anything to eat or drink for five hours.
His IV had been discontinued about half an hour earlier.
"How are you doing, Thomas?" I asked.
"Fine, but I'm thirsty," Thomas said disparagingly.

As a mother, a sharp pain went through my chest.
I had seen many patients who were unable to eat
On time for their CT scans, MRIs, or ultrasounds.
I assured Thomas that the radiology technicians
Would take him down soon.

At 7:10 p.m., I called Thomas. I thought
He would have finished his tests by then.
"No one came to take me," Thomas said weakly.
"It's been more than one hour—and you have
Not eaten or drunk for five or six hours."
I was getting perturbed.

I called the CT scan department and asked about Thomas' CT scan.
They were delayed due to emergency patients from the ER.
I totally understood the urgent situations that take precedence.
I have seen countless auto accidents
And strokes that needed emergency tests immediately.

I regretted calling them and asking when
Thomas would be taken down for his CT scan.
At 7:25, I called Thomas, but he did not answer.
I assumed the x-ray technician had escorted
Him down to the Radiology Department.
About one hour later, I was able to view
All of Thomas's CT scan results.

The chest CT scan showed extensive viral pneumonia,
But his abdomen and pelvis results were clear.
On November,10th morning, five days after
He was admitted, his fever broke.
Later that morning, I talked to Thomas's attending doctor.
Thomas would be discharged that day
With steroids, but he didn't need antibiotics.

What great news! Once they discovered
The source of pneumonia, the fever went away.
I thanked all the doctors profusely
For their excellent care of our Thomas.
"Do you need Dad to pick you up?" I inquired.
"No, I will drive slowly." Tom sounded weak but hopeful.

On his grandmother's birthday, November 10,
He beat the fever and was discharged.
We were thankful that Thomas didn't have COVID-19
And that his pneumonia was on its way to recovery.
During the coronavirus pandemic, it was a challenging event.
I appreciated the divine healing blessing,
And I prayed that the people who were affected
By Coronavirus would quickly regain
Their strength with healthy outcome.

JANUARY 2, 2021

H-Cuisine

In early November 2020, restaurants were shut down again
Due to the resurgence of COVID-19. We have been taking out
Lunches or dinners from a local restaurant in Monroe.
I have tried practically all the entrees on their menu.

Tom and I sometimes enjoy dining out at
An Italian Restaurant after work or church.
Now even that sit-down meal has been restricted to takeout only.

As I was moseying down the supermarket aisles,
I grabbed a couple cans of Manwich for sloppy joes.
I browsed the meat section and picked up one pound of ground beef.

How hard can it be to cook ground beef
And pour a can of Manwich over it to make a sloppy joe?
Tom likes to have Ruffles potato chips when he eats sloppy joes.

A couple bags of Ruffles were thrown in my shopping cart
As well as lettuce, onions, and shredded mozzarella,
To my surprise, Tom liked the sloppy joe meal.

The next day, I bought spaghetti noodles and Prego sauce.
How difficult would it be to pour sauce over noodles?
Again, the supper was a success.

Gradually, my husband's satisfactory meals began to
Build confidence in me to explore further in
Making dinners at home. Therefore, the new
"H-Cuisine" restaurant was opened at my house.

Making Pizza with Mrs. Pezzino

Five cups of two different wheat flours were mixed with one and a half
Tablespoons of yeast, a pinch of salt, and quarter cup of olive oil.
Warm water was poured into the flour
To make the right dough consistency.

Mrs. Pezzino told me to cover it tightly with plastic wrap.
"The secret to making good pizza is to let the dough rise gradually."
This is similar to life; we cannot rush the four seasons,
The ripening of a peach, the growth of a child, or the sunrise.

After two hours, the dough had risen to the top of the pan.
I dug my hands into the soft dough to knead it, fold it right and left,
And turn it upside down. Then I let it rise for another hour.

In the meantime, the sliced pepperoni
And mozzarella were set aside.
To enhance the taste, she told me to sauté the broccoli and mushrooms,
And the onions and green peppers were mixed
With olive oil and dried oregano.

The risen dough was transferred to a rectangular, cooking sheet.
When I was spreading the dough,
It kept retracting—and was not able to fill the corners.

"Aha!" Mrs. Pezzino corrected my hands to press down
On the dough evenly rather than stretching it.
Sure enough, as I was putting my fingerprints on the dough,
The corners remarkably fit like designer clothing.

She opened the homemade tomato sauce
And poured it over the pizza dough.
All the ingredients were strewn on the dough creating a dish fit for a king.
Immediately out of the oven, each bite tasted exquisite.

It was a perfect blend on a crispy, baked crust.
I cherish these moments with Mrs. Pezzino as she taught me
How to make Italian gourmet—and the secret to happiness of life.

Acknowledgments

First and foremost, thank you, Tom, my husband, for always believing in me. Over the past ten years, you whisked me to beautiful Montreal, Toronto, and London, Canada, where most of the poems in my book were written. Although we met only three times before our marriage, the past thirty-five years have been the most enchanting and joyous times of my life.

To my son Matthew, I owe overflowing thanks for reading all my poems and essays as well as giving me invaluable, stimulating new ideas to write.

Abundant thanks to my mother, Chi Sun Rhee, an author of eight books, for emphasizing the power of words and teaching me persistence in writing.

I'm grateful to my father, Sung Hi Rhee, for inspiring me and drilling this idea into my head: "Tigers leave their skin, and men leave books when they die for their legacy."

I thank my other sons and their wives, Thomas, James and Ashley, and Andrew and Ashley, for their enthusiasm and encouragement, as their stories are intertwined in my book.

I thank my instructors and friends at Monroe Martial Arts for teaching me karate techniques and mental discipline, especially Mr. and Mrs. Werner, Mr. Coury, Mr. Delaney,

Mr. Silman, Mrs. Berry, Mr. Clark, Mrs. Ackerman, Mr. Grassley, Ms. Sams, Mr. Hoffer, Mr. Woodfil, Mr. Tedora, Ms. Dakota T., and many more.

I thank my relatives and friends, including Parag Humbad, for inspiring me to take the first step in starting this book. I thank Kay, my high school friend, for your indelible kindness, and Mrs. Betty Pezzino for your cooking lessons and spiritual advice.

I appreciate Alan and Vonnie for being our dinner companions and Bob and Judy Sacka for reading all my writings.

Many thanks to my office staff for helping me care for our patients, so I could concentrate on writing many essays in my spare time. I thank Wendy Pezzino for introducing WestBow Press to publish my book. Overwhelming thanks to the WestBow Press staff and editors for combing through my book with great advice, ideas, and support. This book could not have been possible without all the people I mentioned above and many more.

February 5, 2021

Conclusion

During the past ten years, Tom took me to Montreal, Toronto, and London, Canada. Before these trips, Tom and I had only traveled locally between Michigan and Ohio with our four sons. These family trips to places such as Cedar Point, Sea World, Frankenmuth, Put-In-Bay, and Erie Orchards made wonderful memories as our children grew. Now these boys are grown and have moved out of our house. Two sons are married, and we have a two-year-old grandson. Two other sons have their own jobs and are living independently.

Riding VIA Rail through Canada opened new opportunities for seeing beautiful meadows, scintillating lakes, saffron sunrises, and winter wonderlands. Visiting Toronto was like experiencing New York's Times Square; walking through Old Montreal cobblestone streets was as if we were in Paris; watching *Mary Poppins* and *Cats* on the Grand Theatre stage in London, Ontario, was surreal. It felt like our dreams were coming true.

I wanted to capture these magical moments in poetic form, quickly showcasing their delightful essence. After our trips to Canada, I started to write short poems or essays reminiscing over the incredible and ordinary moments we experienced.

As I was writing these poems, I searched for special event essays that I have written in the past. The first event that came to my mind was when I could not break my board in my early karate class. My heart was pounding even as I recalled the event. Eight years of rigorous karate training brought back exciting and perspiring memories even when I broke my finger.

To maintain physical fitness, I attend six o'clock aerobic classes three mornings a week and swim laps on Saturday mornings at our local YMCA. A remarkable friendship developed with YMCA aerobics class members such as Michelle, Ann, Tom G., Betty, Cathy, and many more. These classes were our wake-up call, and when we were done, we were ready to face any challenges that day.

Countless friends, relatives, and patients have impacted my life in a positive way—these people touched my vitality and journey of enlightenment. They gave me a source of energy and love to move forward in achieving the greater good.

In my Monroe Martial Arts, we started each class by pledging these black belt tenets:

courtesy, integrity, perseverance, self-control, indomitable spirit, modesty, humility, gratitude, and compassion. Even though we are human beings and far from perfect, I tried to follow these codes as much as I could.

CPSIA information can be obtained
at www.ICGtesting.com
Printed in the USA
LVHW031522060921
697122LV00006B/205